May–August 2024

Edited by **Rachel Tranter** and **Olivia Warburton**

BRF Ministries

15 The Chambers, Vineyard
Abingdon OX14 3FE
+44 (0)1865 319700 | brf.org.uk

Bible Reading Fellowship is a charity (233280)
and company limited by guarantee (301324),
registered in England and Wales

ISBN 978 1 80039 260 1

This edition © Bible Reading Fellowship 2024
Cover image © Brushinkin paintings/stock.adobe.com

Distributed in Australia by:
MediaCom Education Inc, PO Box 610, Unley, SA 5061
Tel: 1 800 811 311 | admin@mediacom.org.au

Distributed in New Zealand by:
Scripture Union Wholesale, PO Box 760, Wellington
Tel: 04 385 0421 | suwholesale@clear.net.nz

Acknowledgements
Scripture quotations marked with the following acronyms are taken from the
version shown. Where no acronym is given, the quotation is taken from the version
stated in the contributor's introduction. NASB: New American Standard Bible®,
Copyright © 1960, 1971, 1977, 1995, 2020 by The Lockman Foundation. All rights
reserved. NRSV: New Revised Standard Version Updated Edition. Copyright © 2021
National Council of Churches of Christ in the United States of America. Used by
permission. All rights reserved worldwide. NIV: The Holy Bible, New International
Version® Anglicized, NIV® Copyright © 1979, 1984, 2011 by Biblica, Inc.® Used by
permission. All rights reserved worldwide. KJV: The Authorised Version of the Bible
(The King James Bible), the rights in which are vested in the Crown, reproduced by
permission of the Crown's Patentee, Cambridge University Press.

Every effort has been made to trace and contact copyright owners for material used
in this resource. We apologise for any inadvertent omissions or errors, and would
ask those concerned to contact us so that full acknowledgement can be made in
the future.

A catalogue record for this book is available from the British Library

Printed by Gutenburg Press, Tarxien, Malta

Suggestions for using *Guidelines*

Set aside a regular time and place, if possible, when and where you can read and pray undisturbed. Before you begin, take time to be still and, if you find it helpful, use the BRF Ministries prayer on page 6.

In *Guidelines*, the introductory section provides context for the passages or themes to be studied, while the units of comment can be used daily, weekly or whatever best fits your timetable. You will need a Bible (more than one if you want to compare different translations) as Bible passages are not included. Please don't be tempted to skip the Bible reading because you know the passage well. We will have utterly failed if we don't bring our readers into engagement with the word of God. At the end of each week is a 'Guidelines' section, offering further thoughts about, or practical application of, what you have been studying.

Occasionally, you may read something in *Guidelines* that you find particularly challenging, even uncomfortable. This is inevitable in a series of notes which draws on a wide spectrum of contributors and doesn't believe in ducking difficult issues. Indeed, we believe that *Guidelines* readers much prefer thought-provoking material to a bland diet that only confirms what they already think.

If you do disagree with a contributor, you may find it helpful to go through these three steps. First, think about why you feel uncomfortable. Perhaps this is an idea that is new to you, or you are not happy about the way something has been expressed. Or there may be something more substantial – you may feel that the writer is guilty of sweeping generalisation, factual error, or theological or ethical misjudgement. Second, pray that God would use this disagreement to teach you more about his word and about yourself. Third, have a deeper read about the issue. There are further reading suggestions at the end of each writer's block of notes. And then, do feel free to write to the contributor or the editor of *Guidelines*. We welcome communication, by email, phone or letter, as it enables us to discover what has been useful, challenging or infuriating for our readers. We don't always promise to change things, but we will always listen and think about your ideas, complaints or suggestions. Thank you!

To send feedback, please email **enquiries@brf.org.uk**, phone **+44 (0)1865 319700** or write to the address shown opposite.

Writers in this issue

Andrew Boakye is lecturer in religions and theology at the University of Manchester and co-chair of the Paul Seminar of the British New Testament Society. He is the author of *Death and Life: Resurrection, restoration and rectification in Paul's letter to the Galatians* (Pickwick, 2017).

Rosalee Velloso Ewell is a theologian from São Paulo, Brazil. She is director of church relations for the United Bible Societies and former principal of Redcliffe College. Rosalee lives with her family in Birmingham, UK.

Rachel Tranter is editorial manager at BRF Ministries and co-editor of *Guidelines*. She has a certificate in mission from Cliff College, Derbyshire, and lives in Oxfordshire with her twin sister.

Bill Goodman encourages and enables lifelong learning among clergy and other church leaders in the Anglican diocese of Sheffield, UK. *Yearning for You* is the published version of his Sheffield PhD: a conversation between the Psalms, Song of Songs and contemporary songs, about desire for intimacy.

John Rackley is a Baptist minister who writes for both BRF *Guidelines* and *Bible Reflections for Older People*. He is in ministry with the Christchurch Methodist-Baptist LEP in Leicester and also acts as a consultant and supervisor for various spiritual direction networks. He is currently working on the relationship between narrative and theology.

Helen Paynter is a Baptist minister and tutor in biblical studies at Bristol Baptist College. She is also the founding director of the Centre for the Study of Bible and Violence (**csbvbristol.org.uk**).

Stephanie Addenbrooke Bean is a graduate of Yale University (BA) and Yale Divinity School (MDiv). She was a finalist in the 2022 Theology Slam.

Walter Moberly is emeritus professor of theology and biblical interpretation at Durham University. He has recently written *The Bible in a Disenchanted Age: The enduring possibility of Christian faith* and *The God of the Old Testament: Encountering the divine in Christian scripture* (both Baker Academic).

Ian Paul is a theologian, biblical scholar and local church leader in the Church of England. After a decade in pastoral ministry and another in theological education, he now writes and teaches freelance, publishing at the widely read blog **psephizo.com**.

Ruth M. Bancewicz is church engagement director at The Faraday Institute for Science and Religion, Cambridge. The other contributors to her notes are members of The Faraday Institute or related organisations.

The editors write...

Every new issue of *Guidelines* brings us something new to appreciate. I hope you're looking forward to the notes that are to come. Here is a small taster.

Bill Goodman continues his deep dive into the Psalms, this time guiding us through Book IV (Psalms 90—106). Walter Moberly also finishes off his series on 1 Samuel to take us to the end of the book.

Some new series will also begin in this issue. New writer Andrew Boakye starts his two-part series on Galatians. We also return to our regularly scheduled series on the gospels, with Rosalee Velloso Ewell kicking us off with three weeks on the gospel of Luke. These three-part series, running throughout the year, will now have a different writer for each issue to give us different perspectives and voices.

Rounding off our Old Testament notes, Helen Paynter, former *Guidelines* editor, brings a new perspective on 1 and 2 Kings by looking at these books through the lens of humour. Humour is a truth-seeking device, so what can we learn from it?

We have a further two new writers in this issue. Stephanie Addenbrooke Bean guides us through thinking about work and rest, using Matthew's gospel. She suggests that rest in Jesus is possible, even necessary, as we work (whatever that may look like). I (Rachel) make my writing debut for *Guidelines* looking at the topic of physical disability in the Bible. I aim to challenge ableist interpretations and show how the Bible can be liberating both for those with disabilities and for those who are (currently) able-bodied.

We round off the issue with three more theme-based reflections. Ruth Bancewicz brings a new team of writers to *Guidelines* with challenging and topical notes on creation care. Ian Paul looks at the often-neglected subject of eschatology, telling us to be 'pleasantly surprised' by what we might find! Finally, John Rackley offers a fascinating series on mountains of God, looking at encounters and epiphanies on mountaintops and showing how they act as images of our faith journey with the God of the 'high place'.

We hope these notes will nourish and sustain you as you continue to study scripture with the aim of drawing closer to God.

Rachel   *Olivia*

The prayer of BRF Ministries

Faithful God,
thank you for growing BRF
from small beginnings
into the worldwide family of BRF Ministries.
We rejoice as young and old
discover you through your word
and grow daily in faith and love.
Keep us humble in your service,
ambitious for your glory
and open to new opportunities.
For your name's sake.
Amen.

Helping to pay it forward

As part of our Living Faith ministry, we're raising funds to give away copies of Bible reading notes and other resources to those who aren't able to access them any other way, working with food banks and chaplaincy services, in prisons, hospitals and care homes.

'This very generous gift will be hugely appreciated, and truly bless each recipient… Bless you for your kindness.'

'We would like to send our enormous thanks to all involved. Your generosity will have a significant impact and will help us to continue to provide support to local people in crisis, and for this we cannot thank you enough.'

If you've enjoyed and benefited from our resources, would you consider paying it forward to enable others to do so too?

Make a gift at **brf.org.uk/donate**

Galatians (part I)

Andrew Boakye

Greek philosophy was consumed with the question 'How do I live a good life?' In the 21st-century west, a more pressing question seems to be 'Who am I?' Remarkably, both questions intricately converge in Paul's letter to the Galatians.

Whether the 'Galatians' were ethnic Gauls or a multi-ethnic group living in Roman Galatia, we know that Paul happened upon some Gentile or pagan 'Galatians' (Galatians 4:8–9) as he evangelised Asia Minor. He made a pitstop due to an illness and shared the good news of Jesus the Messiah (Galatians 4:13).

After Paul's departure, unknown believing Jewish missionaries infiltrated the Galatian house churches insisting that Gentiles be circumcised to qualify as the covenant people of God (Genesis 17:10–14). Being circumcised, however, meant embracing the entire Torah (Galatians 5:3; compare James 2:10; 4 Maccabees 5:20–21). The infiltrators also questioned Paul's apostolic credentials. In Galatians, we have Paul's rebuttals.

Paul was commissioned directly by the risen Messiah and reasoned that trusting the risen Messiah was the sole requirement for membership in God's family. This was confirmed by the charismatic activity of the Spirit in the community (Galatians 3:5). Trusting the Messiah was the basis of an experience with God's Spirit, by which a person was re-enlivened with the life of the new age (that is, justified) apart from the works of the Torah.

The apostle thus raises two questions. The first question is the one thing Paul wanted to learn from his audience – did they receive the Spirit by observing the Torah or by responding to the gospel with trust (3:2)? The second question emerges inevitably from Paul's argument – 'Why the Law then?' (Galatians 3:19). These questions intertwine to open a window on the twinned philosophical speculations – *who am I and how do I live a good life?*

Unless otherwise stated, Bible quotations are taken from the NASB.

1 This present evil age

Galatians 1:1–10

Any time we read Paul, our appraisal of his writings operates at (at least) two levels. Initially, there are the specific 'on the ground' issues which occasioned the writing. The second level is the methods and motifs by which the remedy for those issues connect to the broader narrative of God repairing a broken world, climaxing in the Christ event. In the uncharacteristically abrupt and uncongenial opening of Galatians, we are given preliminary hints of both.

On the ground, a quasi-gospel has appeared, to which some in the community are turning, at the behest of some unidentified harassers (vv. 7–8). These outsiders have most likely accused Paul of peddling a soft gospel to curry favour with the Galatian Gentiles (v. 10). In his determination to show he has not been influenced by anyone, Paul opens the letter with a firm stress on the divine origins of the gospel he disseminated among the Galatians (v. 1). However, at the second level, not only was Paul divinely commissioned (v. 1), but the Messiah he proclaimed 'gave himself... so that he might rescue us from this present evil age' (v. 4) – and what more profound image could there be for this rescue than God raising the Messiah from death to new life?

When Paul digresses from standard Greco-Roman epistolary conventions, there are important literary-theological reasons for doing so. The three major deviations from his usual letter openings all impact how the argument of Galatians unfolds. First, rather than 'sender – recipient', Galatians begins 'sender – those who did not send me'! It seems the origins and substance of Paul's gospel were under scrutiny. Second, the identification of God as the one 'who raised [Jesus] from the dead' is central to Galatians, as the apostle will at key moments in the letter define God's work in terms of crucifixion and new life (Galatians 2:19–21; 5:24–25; 6:14–15) and depicts the limitation of the Torah as its inability to generate new life (3:21). The third excursion is the apocalyptic representation of the Christ event in Galatians 1:4. Elsewhere, Paul narrates Jesus' death as 'for our sins' (1 Corinthians 15:3), but in verse 4, the crucifixion is part of a cosmic rescue mission, whereby those trusting the Messiah enter the new age of God's redemptive calling. God delivered Jesus from death to life; now, through Jesus, God delivers believing humanity from deadness to newness.

2 The apocalypse of the Messiah

Galatians 1:11–18

The Pharisees get a raw deal in Christian circles, largely because of their conflicts with Jesus in the canonical gospels (although, as Hyam Maccoby rightly observed, Jesus' Judaism was probably closest to the Pharisees). As a party, Pharisees were committed to their ancestral traditions, especially for interpreting the Torah. Paul considered himself an exemplary Pharisee, 'zealous' in guarding his ancestral traditions (Galatians 1:14).

By the first century AD, 'zeal' was effectively a technical term for the passionate defence of the Torah against socio-religious compromise. It is likely Paul's haranguing of the Jesus movement stemmed from his belief that they were Torah compromisers. The paradigm for this 'zeal' was Phinehas, who murdered an Israelite and his Midianite lover for engaging in an outlawed tryst and was praised for his 'zeal' (Numbers 25:1–13). When, in the mid-second century BC, the Maccabean family resisted the enforced Hellenisation of King Antiochus IV, one of their leaders, Mattathias, also violently defended the Torah. One of the king's officers was indoctrinating an Israelite to make a pagan sacrifice on the altar of a temple in Modien, Judea, and Mattathias killed both the Israelite and the officer. Mattathias is said to have 'burned with zeal for the law, just as Phinehas did' (1 Maccabees 2:26, NRSV).

Unsurprisingly then, the Jerusalem rumour mill went into overdrive – the man who ruthlessly bullied us is now preaching our message (1:23)! According to Luke, Paul had a frosty welcome in Jerusalem – only Barnabas assumed that Paul had laudable motives (Acts 9:26–27).

Whatever happened on the Damascus Road was the turning point of Paul's existence. Did he receive a divine call to service like one of Israel's prophets (Galatians 1:15; compare Jeremiah 1:5)? We most likely do not have the precise language to fully capture what occurred, but we do know that a great unveiling ensued. It was revealed to Paul that the crucified leader of the Nazarene sect was alive in a new way, raised from death to life by the same God Paul believed he served his entire life. Paul accepted that Jesus the Nazarene was Israel's Messiah; consequently, nothing could ever be the same again!

3 The truth of the gospel (1)

Galatians 2:1–10

The proximity and precision with which Paul uses the phrase 'the truth of the gospel' in Galatians 2 demonstrate that it is more than religious shorthand for the authenticity of the gospel message. In verses 5 and 14, Paul labours to ensure that the truth of the gospel is neither violated nor compromised. In both cases, certain parties are guilty of marginalising Gentile Christ believers, and this cuts to the heart of Galatians. The letter addresses the inconsistency between ethnic marginalisation and the good news of Jesus. In the situations reflected in verses 1–5 and 11–14, were Paul not to resist the marginalisation, it would be potentially catastrophic for the community. He unapologetically registers his indifference towards rank in the Jerusalem leadership administration and even suggests that God shares his indifference! He asserts in verse 6 that God shows no partiality, using a Greek phrase that literally means 'God does not receive the face of a man'. The implication is that no one can persuade or impress God by showing him their faultless face.

In verses 1–5, Paul recounts the trip to Jerusalem whereupon he outlined the substance of the gospel he preached among non-Jews. At this meeting, some 'pseudo-brethren' attempted to coerce Paul's Greek co-missionary Titus into being circumcised. Paul did not concede an inch to their demands (v. 6), so 'the truth of the gospel' remained intact.

The resonances between this episode and the following one in Antioch are unmistakable. Both follow on the heels of Paul's account of his own marginalisation of the nascent Jesus community, whom he harassed and marginalised. These three episodes form the critical backdrop for the thesis statement of Galatians – the basis for justification before God – and this ought to give us pause to think through our understanding of what justification means. If Paul's initial mention of 'justification by faith' is contextualised by his attempt to maintain the truth of the gospel by resisting ethnic marginalisation, then any reading of justification as 'how to get saved by a gracious God' (à la Martin Luther) must be read against this background.

4 The truth of the gospel (2)

My father described the strangeness of acclimatising to 1960s London having left West Africa. It was variously hostile, welcoming and awkward when he misread local customs – but it was always *strange*. From our removed vantage points, the strange dynamics involved in assimilating Gentiles into a Jewish messianic movement are easily missed, but they must be recovered.

The major scandal for Gentiles entering the covenant was surrendering allegiance to idols (e.g. 1 Thessalonians 1:9). From domestic idols in one's kitchen, to the Greco-Roman pantheon itself, to the worship demanded by some emperors (the 'cultus'), idolatry was woven into the fabric of imperial life. Citizens generally held that natural disaster, political instability or personal failure meant that the gods needed placating. Pouring libations to household deities and attending public festivals devoted to the gods both prospered and protected the land.

Nonetheless, Rome's typically shrewd political leaders knew they might one day need support from its sizeable Jewish population, for whom idol worship was anathema. So, they compromised – Jews were exempt from worshipping the gods but needed to pray to Yahweh *for* the empire. Furthermore, Rome did not distinguish between Jewish sects. When the Nazarene sect appeared, it was one more Jewish splinter group, entitled to the same exemptions as the other Jews.

However, Gentiles, who were *not* exempt from the cultus or the festivals, started joining the Jesus movement through Paul's ministry, claiming that Jesus embodied Yahweh and expecting the same privileges as the Jews. This was certainly not on the menu! Imagine a Gentile Christ-believer living in a predominantly Gentile housing complex and abstaining from the local festivals. The neighbourhood would question their loyalty and patriotism – why would they not come and worship Artemis or Apollo? Didn't they want to see the city prosper?

Thus, Jewish believers faced pressure from Rome not to encourage Gentiles to abandon the gods *and* from the synagogue not to fraternise with Gentiles, risking Rome revoking Jewish exemptions. When Peter withdrew from the mixed table at Antioch 'fearing those from the circumcision' (v. 12), his fears were legitimate. Evidence suggests that Jewish vigilantes even violently resisted Jewish believers consorting with Gentiles. Paul was unflinching in his judgement that these Jewish believers had erred – but was he right?

5 The truth of the gospel (3)

When Martin Luther nailed his 'Disputation on the power and efficacy of indulgences' to the gates of Wittenberg Castle Church in 1517, he was challenging the notion that salvation could emerge from human striving. He saw in Romans and Galatians ideal analogues for what he understood to be the chief quandary within papal salvation ideology. Luther's first two theses read as follows:

1 When our Lord and Master Jesus Christ said, 'Repent' (Matthew 4:17), he willed the entire life of believers to be one of repentance.
2 This word cannot be understood as referring to the sacrament of penance, that is, confession and satisfaction, as administered by the clergy.

The great reformer connected the sacrament of penance to what Paul called 'works of the law' – both were human-driven attempts to circumvent the guilt of sin – and Galatians had the remedy. Faith, and not works, acquitted a sinner in the divine law court; repentant faith, and not a pardon purchased from a priest, was how sinners found grace from God. This was how Luther understood the phrase 'we are justified by faith and not by the works of the law' (see 2:16). As revolutionary as this appears, it remains to ask whether Paul's objectives and questions were the same as Luther's.

We ended the previous reflection asking if Paul's attack on Peter and the other Antiochene Jewish believers was reasonable. Paul had himself harassed and marginalised Christ-believers in Jerusalem and was stopped in his tracks by the risen Christ himself. He then saw his Greek colleague Titus being marginalised by pseudo-brothers in Jerusalem; the Pauline entourage resisted their demands lest the truth of the gospel be compromised. Gentile believers at Antioch were marginalised by the Jewish believing contingent and Paul blew his top, for, again, the truth of the gospel was in jeopardy. If social marginalisation really betrayed gospel truth, then Paul was right. For now, we may acknowledge the following.

In the verses after the Antioch incident, Paul first introduces the key terminology. Contextually, Pauline assertions about justification by faith in Christ apart from works of the law did not emerge from debates about sinners finding a gracious God, but over whether ethnic marginalisation compromises the truth of the gospel. Once we consider this, we can ask whether Luther's central concerns were the same as Paul's.

6 Trusting the Messiah

Scholars broadly accept that Galatians 2:15–21 is one cohesive unit that flows naturally from v. 14 as a theoretical rebuke of Peter. One must imagine the unit as what Paul would have said to Peter at Antioch, adapted for the Galatian Gentiles.

The 'we' (v. 15) refers to Peter and Paul; a paraphrase of the challenge would say: 'You and I, Peter, are Jews raised on the Torah, not godless heathen living morally dissolute lives. Yet even as law-observant Jews, we know that a person is not 'justified' by the 'works of law' but by *Pistēōs Christou*'.

The three terms in inverted commas are hotly contested. Only limited analysis is possible here, but readers may consult longer treatments from the reading list.

The origins of the word 'justified' are less ambiguous in Greek than English. The Greek noun *dikaiosunē* is normally translated 'righteousness'; the adjective *dikaios* is usually rendered 'righteous'. The Greek verb *dikaioō* is clearly related to the noun and adjective. However, the English verb in most New Testament translations is 'justify' and is not semantically connected to 'righteousness' or 'righteous'. In older English, the noun, adjective and verb might be rendered 'justice', 'just' and 'justify'. As English developed, these terms tended to refer to law-court settings. There are places where Pauline justification language sounds like law-court language, but justification ought to reflect a 'putting right' – it could be a declaration of righteousness, a consideration of righteousness or a transformation into righteousness. We may interpret 'justify' as 'put right in the eyes of God'.

The debates over 'works of the law' (Greek, *erga nomou*) ask if it implies all human striving, all the demands of the Torah, or only those demands forming boundary markers between Jew and Gentile. Again, we will not attempt to settle the question. Nothing in Galatians points directly to all human striving. Even if all the works of the Torah are implied, in Galatians, specific focus is on circumcision, dietary restrictions and sabbath observance, which all uniquely codify Jewish ethnicity.

Pistēōs Christou can legitimately be translated to reflect the believers' trust in Christ or *Christ's faithfulness directed towards God*. Here we will opt for a somewhat central path – the term should be understood as the believers' trust in Christ's own faithfulness, which we will simply call 'Christ-faith'. The believers' trust in the Messiah's faithfulness puts them in the right before God.

Guidelines

Paul has described three occasions of minority marginalisation. Having recounted his own harassment of the nascent Jesus community in Jerusalem (1:13–14), he goes on to narrate the attempt of some false brothers to intimidate his Greek co-missionary Titus into being circumcised (2:1–5). He relates one last marginalisation drama in 2:11–14, where the arrival of some conservative Jewish colleagues of James the brother of Jesus causes Peter, Barnabas and other Christian Jews to hold themselves aloof from a mixed meal table in Syrian Antioch. It is this final incident which forms the immediate literary context for the thesis statement of Galatians: no one is justified by observing the works of the Torah – one is only justified by trusting in the Messiah (2:16).

- Though Paul's apostolic credentials were being questioned, he utterly maintained a refusal to people-please or place leaders on pedestals (1:10; 2:6). How might such an approach promote healthy relationships within Christian community?

- Justification language arises because of the incongruity between exclusivist marginalisation and the gospel; indeed, such marginalisation violates the truth of the gospel (2:5, 14). Where have you experienced marginalisation within Christian community based on ethnicity, gender or social class? How, if at all, was it addressed and did it yield reconciliation?

- Reflect on how Galatians might inform an ethic of social unity which both encourages intra-community harmony and challenges racial and gender-based discrimination.

1 The crucifixion of identity (1)

Galatians 2:17–18

In Galatians 2:16, Paul suggests that no one is put right in the eyes of God by observing Torah and reinforcing Jewish ethnicity, but rather that it is Christ-faith that does so.

An inevitable question emerges from this: if Paul's scheme is incorrect and Christ-faith requires augmenting by the works of the Torah, isn't Paul sinning by discouraging commitment to them? Moreover, if Paul acts on the Messiah's authority, is the Messiah leading Israel into sin?! This is the speculative, rhetorical question in verse 17, which Paul heads off with his trademark emphatic denial, *mē genoitō* ('No way!' or 'Absolutely not!' in colloquial English).

It is also a typical Pauline move to explain why sternly denying a particular proposition is meritorious. Paul attempts this in verse 18, which almost functions in a literary parallel with verse 17; if Paul were to rebuild those things which he has just torn down, *only then* would he be a sinner. *But what exactly has he torn down?* The answer will be expanded in the next two verses, signalled by the explanatory 'for' (*gar* in Greek) at the beginning of verse 19. The paradigm which Paul has deconstructed clearly has something to do with a commitment to the Torah, as will be spelled out in verses 19–20, but it is necessary to clarify the sense in which Paul deconstructed a commitment to the works of the Torah which he must now not rebuild.

For now, it suffices to say that we are about to wade into very stormy waters! Of the questions emerging from his letters, those about Paul's perception of his own ethnic identity and ongoing commitment to the law of Moses are perhaps the thorniest and most difficult to navigate. However one positions oneself regarding these questions, one thing is clear: Paul does not believe that Jewish ethnicity is a pathway to being in right standing before God. In Romans 3:28, the apostle similarly concludes that someone is put right in God's eyes through Christ-faith not legal works. The explanatory inferences in Romans 3:29–30 stem from acknowledging that God is God of Jews and Gentiles alike. Accordingly, human redemption could not rely on a Judeo-centric paradigm (as Galatians 2:17–18). The controversial explanatory verses in Galatians 2:19–20 involve what I am calling the 'crucifixion of identity'.

2 The crucifixion of identity (2)

Galatians 2:19–20

Paul routinely uses the death and suffering of Jesus as an interpretive lens. Far less attention is given to how Paul joins death and life together as an interpretive stencil. For example, in 2 Corinthians 1, Paul describes a harrowing event in Asia as 'death', and God's rescue from it as 'new life'. In Galatians, the twinned motifs of crucifixion and new life are critical to the apostle's articulation of justification.

Three times in Galatians, Paul employs the language and imagery of crucifixion and new life to depict justification. In 5:24–25, Gentiles have 'crucified the flesh' and now live by the Spirit. In 6:14–15, the cosmos suffers crucifixion and emerges in the new creation. In 2:19–20a, Paul says something shocking for any first-century Jew to utter: 'For through the Law I died to the Law, so that I might live for God. I have been crucified with Christ.'

Through the law – Paul consistently labours to demonstrate that the Christ event is both blueprinted in the scriptures, whilst simultaneously a 'bolt from the blue'.

I died to the law – Paul declares himself dead to the very thing which once gave him life and identity.

In order that – this death to the law is the cause of a specific effect.

I might live to God – like Galatians 5:24–25 and passages like Luke 20:38, where Abraham, Isaac and Jacob 'live to God', the term 'live' does not refer to ethical reformation, but to a new kind of existence. The old Paul has died in order to be alive in unique fashion; but consider how 2:19 connects to 2:20: 'And it is no longer I who *live*, but Christ *lives* in me; and the life which I now *live* in the flesh I *live* by faith in the Son of God, who loved me and gave Himself up for me' (Galatians 2:20, italics added).

The repetition of 'live' points to a clear emphasis – a new kind of life has burst upon the scene through the resurrection of Jesus! So much so that the sentence starts with Paul saying he no longer lives but then ends with Paul saying he now lives by trusting God's Son. The conjoining clause explains all – Messiah lives in me. The Paul once alive because of the law has died and is now enlivened by a remarkable and unparalleled vitality – the resurrection energy of Jesus the Messiah!

3 The origin of the Spirit

Galatians 2:21—3:5

There is often a rhythm to the way that the apostle Paul writes. Consider:

1 'If righteousness comes through the Law, then Christ died needlessly' (2:21).
2 'If the inheritance is based on law, it is no longer based on a promise' (3:18).
3 'If a law had been given that was able to impart life, then righteousness would indeed have been based on law' (3:21).

We may infer:

1 Paul does not think Christ's death was needless, so righteousness does not come through law.
2 The second clause in 3:18 specifies that God granted the inheritance to Abraham based on a promise, so inheritance is not based on law.
3 Paul decries the notion that the law and the promise are at odds in the opening of 3:21; the second clause explains the first. The law and the promise are not antithetical to one another; the law was simply never designed to generate life, whereas the promise was.

The conceptual paradigm linking righteousness, inheritance and promise is the Spirit: by the Spirit the righteousness that comes through faith will ultimately be realised (5:5); by the Spirit we will ultimately inherit the kingdom of God (5:16–21); and the promise is summed up as Spirit (3:14). All Paul wanted the Galatian Gentiles to confront was how they received the Spirit. The Galatian Gentiles had experienced the Spirit of God, but was this by observing the works of the Torah or because they had received the gospel with trust?

The question has been partly answered in 2:16–21; the remaining part is why Paul appeals to Abraham in 3:6. Some have suggested the rogue teachers argued their case by recourse to Abraham, and Paul countered – a plausible suggestion given the charge to Abraham in Genesis 17:10–11 to circumcise all his male descendants. However, in Genesis 17:4–5, the author outlines how Abraham will be the father of many nations. As apostle to the nations, irrespective of the infiltrators' deliberations, recourse to Abraham was unavoidable. We may surmise for now that both Spirit possession and justification naturally follow on from trust and are intimately bound up with one another.

4 Who are the children of Abraham?

My son and I are genetically related but are different in some obvious ways. He is energised by company; I am energised by solitude. He appreciates routine; I feel stifled by it. He sleeps very deeply – I wish I could! These contrasts help me to reflect on what Paul means by the sons of Abraham.

The argument in Galatians 4 concerning Abraham's first two sons begins in 3:6, though, in Galatians 3:6–9, Paul is not directly talking about the physical sons of Abraham. In ancient Jewish thought, the significance of connection to Abraham is pivotal. Paul wrote within this context.

Firstly, Abraham lived in the period before the giving of the law. Consequently, some writers saw Abraham as the first proselyte (convert to Judaism). Others rendered Abraham the first monotheist – Abraham's father, Terah, was an idolater (Joshua 24:2), a richly attested theme in rabbinic tradition (compare *Apocalypse of Abraham* 1–8). For Paul, that Abraham lived before the law's arrival and yet trusted in God proved that being in right relationship with God did not require the Torah. Other Jewish writers tried to explain away Abraham's distance from the law, like Philo, who considered the Torah a codification of that which Abraham did by observing the laws of nature.

Secondly, because Abraham was the Gentile father of Judaism, living in the pre-Torah era, Jewish writers referenced him to explain Judaism to non-Jews – a vocation not dissimilar to Paul's.

Although my son and I are genetically related, we are emotionally different. Our identities are not genetically determined, and this holds for Abraham's descendants. In Genesis 17:5, Abraham is the father of *many* nations. In the synoptic tradition, Jews approaching John the Baptist for baptism were warned of an impending judgement: 'Do not assume that you can say to yourselves, "We have Abraham as *our* father"; for I tell you that God is able, from these stones, to raise up children for Abraham' (Matthew 3:9; compare Luke 3:8; Romans 9:6).

In the same way, the true sons of Abraham are not his genetic descendants, but those trusting as he trusted. Trust (faith) is how one received the Spirit in Galatians 3:1–5, trust is how Abraham entered into right relation with God in verse 6 and trust becomes, essentially, the genetic trait of Abraham's true descendants.

5 The life that ends the curse

The resurrection of Jesus ought to be central in Galatians because of how Paul articulates justification. Having identified God as 'resurrector' (1:1), Paul describes his own transformative experience of justification as crucifixion followed by new mode of existence (Galatians 2:19–21); he applies the same model to the Gentiles (Galatians 5:24–25) and the cosmos (Galatians 6:14–15). The most direct statement in Paul about the limitation of the Torah is in Galatians 3:21 – its incapacity to revivify. So, we see, resurrection informs Galatians and is the interpretive key to the difficult verses in 3:10–13.

The text makes four assertions, two of which are flanked by citations from Deuteronomy. The two middle assertions contain biblical citations centred on the idea of 'life'. The Deuteronomy quote in verse 10, alongside the blessing and curse language, clarify that Paul has been ruminating on Deuteronomy 27—30, particularly chapter 30, in which Moses insists that idolatry will be punished with the curse of exile. Paul never mentions exile; however, the author of Deuteronomy describes the curse of exile as *death* and the blessing of restoration as *life*. It is these metaphors Paul seizes upon.

In Galatians 3:10, Paul says: 'All who are of works of the Law are under a curse', citing Deuteronomy 27:26. The verse he cites in fact pronounces a curse on those who do not abide by the things of the law. However, Paul is speaking *collectively* of Israel's failure to abide by the law and incur the curse of exile and death. Note that Paul states that Christ takes away the curse (v. 13) – in other words, Paul believed that the curse of exile endured right up until the time of Christ; as such, the next two citations take the argument in an interesting direction.

Galatians 3:11 quotes Habakkuk's prophecy of Judah's response to the Babylonian invasion (Habakkuk 2:4). The righteous ones will live, that is, not be destroyed by the Babylonians, by trusting in YHWH. Paul draws upon this language of living to describe those who will place their trust in Messiah. They will live – *overcome the curse of exile – death*. This is confirmed by how Paul describes the nature of the law in verse 12. Finally, Paul reinterprets Deuteronomy 21:23 in verse 13; by taking on the curse of death in crucifixion, Jesus embraced the Deuteronomic curse of death and removed it from Israel.

6 The promise of the Spirit

Galatians 3:14–18

The previous reflection demonstrated that trust (faith) leads to the life which puts one in the right before God and truly ends the exile. That this life comes from trust, and not from law, reminds the reader of the conclusion drawn from 3:1–6. Life is mediated by the Spirit, and the Spirit comes through trust not the law, for the law is not of trust (3:12) and, thus, cannot generate life (3:21).

We ended concluding that Jesus takes the curse of death away from Israel in crucifixion (3:13); this is…

Galatians 3:14a	Galatians 3:14b
in order that	so that
to the Gentiles	we
the blessing of Abraham would come	would receive the promise of the Spirit
in Christ Jesus	through faith

Galatians 3:14 has puzzled scholarship for two reasons – the curse of the law is contrasted with the blessing of *Abraham* and the blessing of Abraham is equated with the promise of the Spirit. In Genesis, Abraham is promised a son, a nation and a territory, but never the Spirit; so, what can Paul mean?

The nation will emerge from Abraham's son Isaac, whose descendants will inherit the promised land. The primordial promise, then, is of a son – the promise Paul says will be credited as righteousness (Genesis 15:6 in Galatians 3:6). The promise is rehearsed in verse 16, which points to a single recipient of the promise. The promise of Spirit will not be conferred on the many offspring (Israel), but the single seed, Messiah. The joint quandaries contained in verse 14 hereby find their resolution.

Equating the promise with the blessing, Paul indicates that the curse of death contrasts the blessing of life. The sense in which the Spirit generates life originates from Genesis 2:7 (compare Ezekiel 37:6, 9). When Galatians 4:29 announces that Isaac was born according to the Spirit, Paul implies that Isaac's birth was a resurrection miracle – as spelled out explicitly in Romans 4:17–25, where Isaac's birth foreshadows the resurrection of Jesus. The promise made to Abraham brought in miraculous new life, manifested in the birth of Isaac according to the promise of God. The promise was made to Abraham and the Messiah (3:16), for the Messiah would also encounter a miraculous experience of new life in his resurrection. Those who are in Christ receive this new life, foretold by Habakkuk, by trust and through the Spirit.

Guidelines

When Paul placed his trust in the risen Messiah, he went through an experience which he likened to the experience of the Christ event – a crucifixion by which he was alive in a new way (Galatians 2:19; later he will interpret the experience of transformed Gentiles and even a transformed cosmos through the same lens). He argues that trust was the basis of Abraham being in right relationship with Israel's God (Galatians 3:6), and that this corresponds to the trust in the gospel which permitted the activity of the Spirit among the Gentiles (Galatians 3:1–5). Having argued that the notion of new life being the result of faith was itself embedded in the scriptures (Galatians 3:7–13), the strands of Paul's defence converge – the promises God made to Abraham are summed up by the Spirit, who is given to people who trust in the Messiah (Galatians 3:14). The addition of the Mosaic law did not in any way alter the parameters of this covenant promise (Galatians 3:15–17).

- Death and resurrection did not just happen *to* Jesus, but it is happening *through* him. When you reflect on a discipleship of 'life bearing' – bringing the energising life of Jesus to arenas of deadness in your own social world – what does that conjure up for you? In what ways might believers through their own lives bring life to others?
- How might the notion of the crucifixion of your identity help you navigate change, growth and maturity in your walk with God?
- Paul speaks ubiquitously of believers being in Christ. He speaks far more seldomly of Christ being in believers, but what might be the significance of acknowledging that 'Christ lives in us'?

FURTHER READING

John Barclay, *Paul and the Power of Grace* (Eerdmans, 2020).

Michael F. Bird, *The Saving Righteousness of God: Studies on Paul, justification and the new perspective* (Wipf and Stock Publishers, 2007).

James D. G. Dunn, *The Epistle to the Galatians (Black's New Testament Commentaries)* (Continuum, 1993).

Neil Martin, *Galatians Reconsidered: Jews, Gentiles, and justification in the first and the twenty-first centuries* (Apollos, 2022).

J. Louis Martyn, *Theological Issues in the Letters of Paul* (T&T Clark International, 1997).

Peter Oakes and Andrew Boakye, *Rethinking Galatians: Paul's vision of oneness in the living Christ* (T&T Clark, 2021).

N. T. Wright, *Galatians (Commentaries for Christian Formation)* (Eerdmans, 2021).

Kent L. Yinger, *The New Perspective on Paul: An introduction* (Cascade Books, 2011).

Luke 1—8

Rosalee Velloso Ewell

Imagine receiving an invitation to go on an incredible journey with some equally incredible people. The gospel of Luke is such an invitation, but with a twist: the cost of the trip has already been paid and any who join along the road are to be welcomed. You must learn a new type of engagement with others that is shaped by the life and love of the guide – Jesus of Nazareth.

We know very little about Luke. Perhaps he had been a companion of Paul on his missionary travels and had learned first-hand what it meant to journey for the sake of the gospel. Early church documents suggest he was a doctor by training (see Colossians 4:14) and he is the author of this gospel and the book of Acts.

One might be tempted to read the gospels, especially Luke's, as if they were modern-day biographies, but that is not the case. While Luke is systematic in the way he crafts the invitation, he highlights only fundamental events and stories that aim to draw his readers in, inviting all people, then and now, to journey with Jesus.

This is not going to be an easy trip. It will follow in the ways God led his people Israel in days of old, even as it looks forward to the new and amazing ways Jesus breaks open the promises of God to include all sorts of different people. In these early chapters, Luke introduces us to some of the main characters, showing how they responded to God's invitation to journey and the obstacles and blessings they faced. As we read the gospel, Luke's question frames the narratives: how will we respond today?

Bible quotations are taken from the NRSV.

1 The Gentile who testifies

Luke 1:1–4

Many scholars agree that the initial verses of this gospel, together with the prologue of Acts, are the most beautifully crafted and perfectly balanced construction of all of Luke—Acts or even of the entire New Testament (see Woodward et al., p. 6). In elegant Hellenistic style, Luke sets out how he gathered evidence for his writing (vv. 2–3), why he decided to write this gospel (v. 4) and to whom it is dedicated (v. 3).

The ancient world had its own versions of 'fake news'. Luke is clear that his account is based on sound investigation and good evidence (vv. 2–3), which he will employ throughout this narrative to explain in an orderly fashion the key moments of Jesus' story. The term he uses for 'a well-ordered account' (v. 3) has the connotation of a journey – he is organising the evidence in such a manner as to take the reader on a life-transforming tour. His reader, Theophilus (v. 3), which means 'lover of God', could either be the distinguished patron of his work or anyone in general who loves God.

Luke was writing at a time of persecution and in a context where those early Christians suffered under the Jewish authorities and under the Romans. He sets out his account of the gospel having witnessed the martyrdom of many of the first disciples and of Paul himself. Perhaps Luke, a Gentile, had come to follow Jesus through the witness of Paul and was made an unlikely record-keeper of the events of the early church.

There is no presumption that Luke's account is the only account of the life of Jesus. Rather, as one who was not an eyewitness to Jesus' life on earth, he relies on accounts of others and on the faithful testimony of those first disciples who were 'servants of the word' (v. 2). He is clearly indebted to them, but even as he looks to the past for reliable evidence, his eye is on the future and the ways Jesus' story can always encourage and empower disciples in all places.

Interestingly, Jesus' name is not mentioned in this introduction. Rather, the journey on which we embark is one of learning what it means to be a disciple of Christ as we gain a 'firm grasp' of the things we have already been taught (v. 4). This is not a journey for the faint-hearted, but one that requires courage, humility and obedience to follow the direction Jesus sets out.

2 The God who surprises

We know from medical research how much of our lives are shaped by our family history, whether we are prone to certain illnesses or react to situations in a particular way. Following the dedication to Theophilus, Luke introduces the readers to part of Jesus' family history, showing the church, then and now, the arc of this great journey with a God who surprises even in the midst of oppression.

The ageing priest Zechariah and his childless wife, Elizabeth, are contrasted with the political power of King Herod (vv. 5–7). In the natural order of things, Herod would have never known of this couple, yet Luke masterfully shows the irony of the contrast between these characters, for it is the future child of Zechariah and Elizabeth who will be the cause of great fear and trouble for King Herod (compare Luke 9:9; Mark 6:14–29).

It is to this old couple – unknown and unremarkable – that God sends his angel to give Zechariah the surprise of his life (v. 11). The text says Zechariah was chosen by lot (v. 9) to enter the sanctuary. As in the choice of Matthias to replace Judas Iscariot (Acts 1:26), the power of God and the discernment in prayer stand behind Luke's portrayal of casting lots. Zechariah is not chosen by chance – he is introduced as a key player who links the journey of Israel with God in the Old Testament to the coming of John the Baptist and Jesus.

The angel's message to Zechariah echoes stories and key figures from Israel's past – Abraham and Sarah or Jacob and Rachel – who also had children when they were older. Yet Zechariah is not portrayed as a great hero of the faith; rather, he is struck speechless for his disbelief in the angel's message (v. 20). The old couple are faithful and devout Jews (v. 6), but they are ordinary people to whom God gives an extraordinary task. Luke emphasises the fidelity of God towards his people, taking away Elizabeth's shame (v. 25) and empowering her son with the Holy Spirit to bring God's people back to God (vv. 16–17) and to prepare the way for the coming of the Messiah (compare 1:76).

3 The girl who obeys

Luke 1:26–56

Perhaps more than any other passage in the New Testament, these two short stories – the angel Gabriel who visits Mary and Mary's subsequent visit to Elizabeth – display the deepest faith and trust in God's love and justice. These two ordinary women, one a young girl and the other an old woman, model for us a faith so powerful that it subverts kings and rulers and overthrows the rich and powerful.

Scholars have often pointed out how Luke's gospel is especially marked by his emphasis on God's calling of women and the empowering of the out-cast or the poor. Far from Herod's palace in Jerusalem, God sends the angel Gabriel (the same one who appeared to Zechariah) to Mary, a girl in Nazareth (vv. 26–27). In contrast to Zechariah's disbelief, the text says Mary is perplexed and ponders the angel's words (v. 29), before submitting in total confidence to what God has asked her to do: 'Here am I, the servant of the Lord; let it be with me according to your word' (v. 38). Not only does Mary accept the task of bearing God's Son, but she also shows no doubt about the miraculous pregnancy of her relative Elizabeth and soon after sets out to visit her (v. 39).

The greetings and songs of praise of these two women have shaped the liturgy and prayers of Christians for many centuries. Sometimes we repeat Elizabeth's words to Mary, 'Blessed are you among women, and blessed is the fruit of your womb' (v. 42), along with Mary's words, 'My soul magnifies the Lord, and my spirit rejoices in God my Saviour' (v. 47), without consider-ing the deeply subversive and amazing power of such praise. Luke is clear that Mary and Elizabeth speak and act in the power of the Holy Spirit (vv. 38, 41). God's favour is shown on two women from the margins of society, who through their obedience are made instruments of God's reign, ushering in the climax of God's journey with his people.

Mary's song is steeped in the words of the psalms and the prophets and is itself a brief description of what it is like to journey with the almighty God. Luke plays with time, mixing past, present and future – though Mary is an unwed pregnant woman, suffering in a community under a foreign empire, she can proclaim God's justice and victory: 'He has brought down the powerful from their thrones and lifted up the lowly' (v. 52). We are invited to learn obedience from Mary and Elizabeth.

4 The women who give birth

The question that all the people ask after the birth of John the Baptist could be seen as the leading question for Luke's entire gospel: "'What then will this child become?' For indeed the hand of the Lord was with him' (1:66). As we journey with Jesus, Luke unfolds for his readers the ways in which God is with both John and Jesus. Luke hints at the power of the Spirit, which Jesus will pass on to his disciples and to all those who believe and obey throughout the world.

Following the order of his introductions of Zechariah and Elizabeth and Joseph and Mary, we are taken to witness the birth of these promised children. Elizabeth's pregnancy had itself testified to God's mercy and justice and was the source of great rejoicing in the community (1:58). Yet even though the people rejoiced, they are doubtful when Elizabeth names her son John (1:61) and need the confirmation from Zechariah, who is still mute because of his own doubting of the angel. Zechariah confirms the name, John, and immediately speaks, praising God with another hymn that has also shaped the liturgy of the church for many centuries.

For about nine months, Zechariah has been on a journey of faith. It is now his turn, many months after Elizabeth was blessed, to be filled with the Holy Spirit (1:67). In a beautiful turn of phrase that parallels Mary's song, Zechariah's prophecy also echoes the psalms and prophets of ancient Israel. God has redeemed his people and set them free to worship him without fear (1:68, 74). John the Baptist, in the heritage of Isaiah, is the one sent to prepare the people to receive the Lord Jesus.

As he turns to the birth of Jesus, Luke contrasts the power of this world – the Roman Emperor Augustus (2:1) – with a manger in the marginal city of Bethlehem (2:4–7). While the emperor's vassal rulers like Herod were busy with a census, a cosmic shift was under way, witnessed not by employees of the empire, but by shepherds and angels. Though at first the shepherds are fearful, they hear the proclamation of Jesus' birth and go 'with haste' to find Mary, Joseph and the child (2:16). They join the journey with God – the only possible outcome is to share this with others (2:17). As she had pondered the angel's first words to her, Mary also ponders these things in her heart (2:19).

5 The children who grow up

Luke 2:22–52

The contrast between the world's power and what comes to us in Jesus is a constant theme in Luke's gospel. The prophetic words of Mary and Zechariah announce the coming victory of God and the freedom of Israel, but as it turns out, it is not the type of kingdom the people were expecting. We see this again in this passage. As Tom Wright suggests, 'This is becoming a story about suffering. Simeon is waiting for God to comfort Israel. Anna is in touch with the people who are waiting... They are both waiting in a world of patient hope, where suffering has become a way of life' (Wright, pp. 25–26).

Luke is keen to show his readers that Jesus and his family were faithful, law-abiding Jews who did what was customary 'in the law of the Lord' (v. 23). Yet even as he draws the connections between Israel's past and its future, he prepares us to expect the unexpected and invites us to find ourselves in the story, journeying (twice) with Mary, Joseph and Jesus to the temple in Jerusalem.

In the first journey (vv. 22–24), the parents take Jesus to be dedicated to the Lord. There they encounter two older people who are both full of the Spirit and who have dedicated themselves to serving God. Luke puts on Simeon's lips another hymn of praise. It is poignant in the way it points towards the end of Simeon's own life – he is dismissed in peace (v. 29) – and in his prophecy to young Mary – 'a sword will pierce your own soul' (v. 35). The themes of surprise and subversion are still evident in this prophecy. From Israel will come the true ruler of the universe and he will draw all nations into himself (vv. 31–32). Yet this is not the type of revelation or redemption that Israel itself was hoping or praying for! In a tender pastoral note, old Anna steps in after Simeon's words to Mary and, like the shepherds before her, spoke about the child to all who lived in hope of redemption (v. 38).

Twice in Luke's gospel we find a couple on the road going away from Jerusalem. Both times Jesus has been lost. In this text, his parents realise the twelve-year-old is missing. In Luke 24, the couple think he is dead. Both times Jesus reveals himself to be more than any had imagined – God surprising us on the journey.

6 The cousins who meet

Life under the brutal Roman rule is the backdrop to the way Luke introduces John the Baptist and his proclamation of the kingdom of God. Like the Christians in Luke's time, the Jews were suffering greatly, and everyone expected (or at least hoped for) an imminent change, even a revolt against the empire. Luke contrasts the details of those in power (vv. 1–2) with the powerful word of God that came to John, son of Zechariah and Elizabeth (vv. 2–3). Keeping with the big arc of God's story, Luke employs the words of Isaiah to place John right in the centre of God's plan for redemption (vv. 4–6). However, the kingdom that John announces does not look like the overthrow of Rome or the restoration of a king like David.

John's message is harsh. He does not mince words in his criticisms of the religious powers or the self-righteous attitude of nearly everyone – even the crowds are called a 'brood of vipers' (v. 7). Even in so challenging a message, there is an invitation to everyone, especially those on the margins, to repent and to bear fruit worthy of God's justice and love. Luke offers us a list of those who asked John for guidance ('What should we do?'): the crowds (v. 10); tax collectors (v. 12); and soldiers (v. 14). To all he says, 'Repent and be baptised', for these are the signs of the journey from judgement to freedom in God.

John's preaching is not lost on the powers of the world, and for his rebuke of Herod and his wife/sister-in-law Herodias, John is imprisoned (vv. 19–20). Only later will the readers find out what happens to John the Baptist, but Luke's message is clear: there is a confrontation between the power of the world and the power of God; those who accept the invitation to journey with God will face the consequences, but in doing so, they will be made heirs to the true kingdom (compare 6:22–23).

Jesus' baptism is marked by the Holy Spirit – the God who empowered Mary now makes himself known in a completely new way through his beloved Son (v. 22). Luke closes the circle of this long introduction with Jesus' genealogy (vv. 23–38), which functions like a drum roll in the scriptures. The list of ancestors ties the story to the past and points to the beginning of the future inaugurated by Jesus. He is the 'son of Adam, son of God' (v. 38).

Guidelines

- Throughout these initial chapters, Luke introduces us to the themes of the justice and power of God contrasted with the ways the world values power, such as the Roman Empire or the wealthy. In today's world, it is often the media who determine what is important or not. In what ways does Luke's gospel speak to these contrasts in our contexts, calling us to a different kind of perspective and worldview shaped by the lowliness of the story of Jesus?

- We have seen how journeys play an important role in this gospel. There is an invitation to answer God's call and to journey with Jesus, through Mary and Joseph, to Bethlehem and to Jerusalem. How can a deeper knowledge of Luke's gospel enable the church today to practise the type of obedience that follows Christ and proclaims his kingdom, even unto death, as did John the Baptist?

- How does Luke's portrayal of the absolute confidence that Elizabeth and Mary have in God challenge us to pay closer attention to those people who are often overlooked in our congregations and society? Could it be that through them we will learn something new about the ways God calls us to journey with Christ?

1 The scandal of inclusion

Luke 4:1–30

It has been said that if we were to cut Jesus, he would bleed the scriptures of Israel. This is perhaps most evident in the narrative of his temptations in the desert (vv. 1–12). Luke continues to take his readers on a journey that recalls Israel's past – the 40 years meandering through the wilderness and their years of captivity in Babylon. The reality facing the young churches in Luke's time was not unlike the oppression that Israel suffered under Pharaoh or the Babylonians. Yet for Luke, it is not the foreign rulers who are the enemy, but Satan himself, who tempts Jesus by exploiting his hunger (v. 3), offering him worldly powers (vv. 5–7) and questioning his status as God's Son (vv. 9–11). At each temptation, Jesus uses the power of God's word to counter the devil's suggestions until at last, the devil 'departed from him until an opportune time' (v. 13).

Luke frequently reminds us that Jesus was filled with the power of the Spirit (compare 3:22; 4:1, 14), who not only enables him to withstand Satan's temptations but also prepares him for the ministry that is to come. From his birth, news about him had been spreading through the testimony of people like the shepherds and Anna. But Luke fast-forwards from Jesus at age twelve in Jerusalem to Jesus as a grown man, preaching and teaching throughout the region, 'praised by everyone' (v. 15).

When he arrives in Nazareth, the town where he had spent at least some of his youth, we find Jesus speaking in the synagogue and teaching from the prophet Isaiah (vv. 17–21). Just at this point, in his home city, Luke introduces a theme that came up only briefly in Zechariah's song: the scandalous inclusion of outsiders into God's promises to Israel. Jesus' sermon is going well, and the people are amazed at his gracious words (v. 22), until he gets to the application of the text – God's grace is extended to a widow from Sidon and to a Syrian general – both outsiders to the people of Israel. Foreshadowing what will come later as Jesus welcomes tax collectors and sinful women, or Peter's encounter with Cornelius (Acts 10), the reaction to his sermon is vitriolic. The people are not ready for all the others whom God calls to join them on this journey. They think they know what it means to be God's people, but Jesus shows them otherwise.

2 When demons proclaim

Luke 4:31–44

Having escaped the angry synagogue-goers in Nazareth, Jesus makes Capernaum, a fishing village on the shores of Lake Tiberias (Sea of Galilee), his centre of operations. This village at the edge of the earth's lowest freshwater lake was also the hometown of the fishermen brothers Peter and Andrew, and James and John. Imagine this little fishing village suddenly filled with people because a celebrity has come to town. This is the snapshot Luke gives his readers – a town overwhelmed with people who have brought their loved ones to be healed of disease and freed of demons.

Yet in the background of Luke's text is the emphasis on Jesus' authority and identity. We first see this with the proclamation of the demon-possessed man, 'What have you to do with us, Jesus of Nazareth?… I know who you are, the Holy One of God' (v. 34). In contrast to the people in Nazareth, it is a frightening thing that a demon recognises Jesus and affirms who he is. His identity as God's Holy One is reaffirmed in the authority with which he rebukes the demons. As Wright points out, most people saw him simply as a prophet, but the reader is shown the reality – he is God's Son (Wright, p. 52). As such, Jesus does not need to employ special formulas or incantations to heal or free people – his power is in his words alone, so a simple 'Come out of him!' (v. 35) suffices. The people are amazed at such authority (v. 36) and reports of this spread throughout the region (v. 37). Jesus continues to proclaim God's reign and to heal many, but his ultimate identity and authority are hidden to most, except the demons, who recognise the Messiah (v. 41) but are silenced by him.

In the ordinary context of a home and an elderly woman with a fever, the reader is introduced to Simon Peter (v. 38), who is destined to become one of the closest disciples of Jesus and a leading figure in the early church. Jesus heals Peter's mother-in-law and immediately she begins serving them (v. 39). Accepting the invitation to follow Christ might mean healing, but it certainly means service. Just as his mother-in-law serves them, so Peter (and those to whom Luke writes) will learn the cost of discipleship and the upside-down kingdom into which Jesus invites them.

3 Shocking partnerships

Luke 5:1–32

After the underwhelming introduction to Simon Peter that we are given in Luke 4, here the story takes a dramatic turn. It is clear from the narrative that Peter wavers between belief and unbelief, probably like most of us. Yet again, Luke's emphasis is both on the authority of Jesus and on the ways people respond to his call to follow.

Jesus is still the celebrity in town and the crowd is pressing in on him (v. 1). Presumably he knows Peter and Andrew, since he healed Peter's mother-in-law, and so the request to use their boat as a pulpit is not out of the blue. Sound carries on water, so Jesus' words to the people might have been heard by all who were on the beach, awaiting the return of this extraordinary healer (v. 3).

Luke highlights the mundane, seemingly pointless tasks of ordinary people and raises them to the status of those used by God. Peter and his friends had a miserable night fishing. The arrival of Jesus presents them with a challenge: to obey this strange man's commands or to go about with life as usual. Peter's response is clear: 'Master… if you say so, I will let down the nets' (v. 5). The Spirit's invitation to join the journey with Jesus is offered to all. The question Luke suggests is whether we will have the ears to hear, as Peter did, to answer the call.

Following the amazing catch of fish, Luke narrates a leper who is healed and a paralytic who is dropped through a roof to be healed by Jesus. This leads to a confrontation with the religious leaders, who question Jesus' authority to heal and forgive (v. 21). But again, the emphasis is on the journey. So soon after asking Peter to join him, Jesus invites Levi, the tax collector. Nothing in their world would bring Peter and Levi together. It was an unimaginable alliance between a fisherman and a tax-collector. But just as Peter accepted the call to follow, so did Levi. Thus, the two would have to learn that to be near Jesus they would have to be near one another. This is the shocking story of being on the road with Jesus – he calls, and we have no control over those to whom the invitation is also extended.

4 New kingdom, new rules

Luke 5:33—6:11

The Pharisees thought they knew what it meant to live as God's chosen people in a society ruled by the Roman Empire. Their laws and regulations were not a matter of thoughtless legalism but were deeply tied up with how they tried to maintain their identity as God's people. When Jesus called the first disciples and healed the leper, he was already crossing boundaries that disrupted the status quo. Here, Luke reinforces the themes of boundaries and borders and the ways these shape a people's identity and sense of being.

Jesus' encounters with the Pharisees highlight the power plays and the challenges of who is considered part of God's people and who is left outside – there are many 'us' and 'them' questions about who needs healing and who does not, whose sins need forgiving and who gets to forgive. Throughout the narrative, Luke shows us how the things that kept the Jewish people together, the rules that defined their collective identity, are disrupted by the arrival of Jesus and his disciples. Yet even as Jesus disrupts, he creates a new space, a new understanding of identity around his very person. Luke is clear that the reason Jesus can do this is his authority as the Son of Man (6:5).

In that society, fasting was a sign of repentance and implied a request to God: 'Please, have mercy on us and rescue us! Restore the kingdom of Israel!' Yet the new kingdom had come in Jesus, even if not in the ways the people of Israel expected. There ought to be feasting and celebrations when a new king comes to the throne; the time of mourning is reserved for when he is gone (5:35). But Luke and his readers know the end of the story – even the time of mourning will be temporary.

Fasting and keeping the sabbath were important markers of the old reign. Like mixing old cloths and new ones, they do not match up – as Wright explains, one cannot fit Jesus' new work into the thought-forms of the old, because this will only lead to an explosion (Wright, p. 65).

Just as David was the rightful king, anointed without pomp or circumstance (compare 1 Samuel 16), so Jesus has come as the climax of that journey of God to his people. He claims authority and sovereignty as he challenges all people to open their eyes, to see the new age that is dawning. It is the kingdom of forgiveness and life (6:9), which can only be offered by God's anointed Son.

5 The teacher and his students

Luke 6:12–26

Until this point in the narrative, we have heard vaguely about some of the characters, such as Simon Peter and Levi, but they remain part of the larger group that follows Jesus around without any specific tasks or assignments. In this passage, the journey takes on an even more serious and sombre tone – after a whole night of praying, Jesus chooses and names twelve disciples to whom he gives the status of 'apostles', which means 'those who are sent'. This is a profound moment in at least two ways: (1) with the exception of Judas Iscariot, these are the ones who will take centre stage in Luke's second volume, Acts, many of whom are martyred; (2) there is the clear claim that their number and naming echoes the calling of the twelve tribes of Israel and the establishment of those whom God has chosen to help usher in the new age.

In Mark's gospel, they are given the job of being with Jesus, preaching and casting out demons (see Mark 3:13–15), but in Luke's narrative they have no such power, yet. Jesus is the supreme healer and preacher. Crowds come from all Judea, Jerusalem and the coastal towns to bring their loved ones for healing and to hear Jesus teach (vv. 17–19). Luke dramatically describes the scene almost as if Jesus were surrounded by a mob, each one wanting some of the power that went out from him and made them well.

The miraculous actions are not divorced from who Jesus is or what he teaches. Rather, each reinforces the other, adding evidence for Luke's readers that this man was the promised Messiah of Israel and Saviour of the world. Luke carefully arranges Jesus' teachings in sets of four – four blessings and four curses – which introduce his disciples to the terms of the new covenant. These are the rules of engagement while on the journey with Christ.

Jesus radically sets out a vision for righting the injustices of the current age. As he said in Nazareth, 'Today this scripture has been fulfilled' (4:21). As the prophets had foretold, the Messiah would bring blessings to the poor, hungry, sad and oppressed (vv. 20b–23), and judgement to those who are complicit in the oppression of others (vv. 24–26). Jesus' words echo the Old Testament prophets and, like them, he and his followers will be persecuted by the powers of this world.

6 The extravagant love of God

The quick succession of short stories in this passage includes a few of the most well-known sayings of Jesus, which for some people may evoke vivid images from children's Bibles – the collapsing house that was built without a good foundation (v. 49) or the man with a huge tree coming out of his eye (v. 41). There is the danger that the familiarity of these stories makes it harder for us to grasp the revolutionary nature of what Jesus is saying and doing.

Luke is careful to show his readers that Jesus is the fulfilment of all God was doing in the past (compare 24:44–49) and all God planned for the redemption of Israel and all creation. These sayings are not to-do lists or moral advice, because life isn't always fair. Jesus is describing for us something fundamental to who God is and what life looks like when one follows the God perfectly revealed in Christ.

God created the world out of love and, even after Adam and Eve had sinned, God lovingly sewed new clothes for them (see Genesis 1—2; 3:21). This extravagant divine love marked the journey of the Lord with his people in the Old Testament – over and over again God forgives their sins and rebellion; God prepares a feast in the presence of their enemies (Psalm 23:5); God has compassion on them despite their ingratitude (Hosea 11; Luke 6:36). Loving our enemies (v. 27), giving to all who ask (v. 30), not judging (v. 37) – these are the rules for journeying with the God who loves us no matter what. Later in the gospel, Luke drives this point home in the story known as 'the prodigal son' (Luke 15).

With a touch of humour (Wright, p. 76), Jesus builds on the stories of generosity to remind his listeners that they need to choose: either the ways of the past – being busy with the smallest matters of the law while missing the big picture of God's love for all – or the way of Jesus, who opens up in himself the manner by which Israel is to be a light to the nations. Luke's readers would know that Jesus' way of life resulted in hate, abuse (v. 28), the stripping of his cloak (v. 29) and ultimately death at the hands of his enemies, whom he forgave and loved (23:34).

Guidelines

- In our churches and communities today, there are many divisions, many ways we exclude 'others' and draw lines between 'us' and 'them'. In what ways might Luke's telling of the boundaries Jesus crossed, or the odd mix of people he chose as his disciples, challenge us to rethink the places and the people we also are called to love?

- Throughout Luke's gospel, Jesus illustrates the ways of God's kingdom by highlighting people, places and things that are discarded by the world: a leper, tax collectors, a Samaritan village. Jesus brings justice to those thrown away by society. Who are the people or places that have been discarded in our society? How is Jesus' reflection of God's extravagant love a renewed call to Christians today?

1 The great healer

Luke 7:1–17

In the previous text we are told that power went out from Jesus and 'healed all of them' (6:19), almost as if such healing power could not help but overflow from Jesus' very person. In contrast, Luke now narrates two miraculous healings in much greater detail, painting a picture for the readers of the context, the main characters and Jesus' own motivations for his actions and words.

Having taught his apostles and any of those who were paying attention the type of love, patience and generosity they needed in order to follow him (v. 1), we find Jesus back in the fishing village of Capernaum, where he had already become a celebrity (4:36–37). Luke gives us a taster of what is to come later in Acts 10, when Peter meets Cornelius. God's abundant love is for all, even Gentiles like this centurion and his dying slave (v. 2). Interestingly, the Jewish elders are the ones who plead on the centurion's behalf, which suggests that these elders were probably not Pharisees but just local leaders who maybe wanted to maintain the good relationship they had with this man who worked for Herod's army. Yet even as Luke describes positively the ways the Jewish elders ask Jesus to heal the centurion's servant, in Jesus' words we see the contrast between the unbelief of the Jews and the faith of the Gentile – 'Not even in Israel have I found such faith' (v. 9).

The town of Nain was about a full day's journey from Capernaum and not too far from Nazareth. Jesus and his companions come upon the funeral procession for a widow's only son as she and the villagers carry her son's body to its final resting place. It is a poignant scene and, in contrast to the centurion's story, no one in this episode displays any profound faith. As a masterful storyteller, Luke couples the raising of the widow's son and the healing of the centurion's slave with the two healings in Jesus' sermon in Nazareth (4:25–27) – God's grace and healing through his prophets extends to two men of power and wealth (Naaman and the centurion) and to two destitute widows, one in Sidon and the other in Nain (1 Kings 17; see also 2 Kings 4). There are no boundaries that contain such love, compassion and power.

Finally, Luke uses the powerful language of the exodus, echoed also in Mary's song, to describe the people's reaction to Jesus' raising the boy to life – 'God has visited his people!' (v. 16).

2 What are you looking at?

Luke 7:18–35

This passage is about politics and the character of the kingdom that God is setting up in and through Jesus. It is also about identity and belonging and how we are able to understand (or not) what it looks like to live under Jesus' rule. The context for John is prison. His prophetic ministry in the wilderness, where he preached repentance and baptised all who came to him (Luke 3), had landed him in prison because of his criticism of Herod's marriage to his brother's wife (3:19–20; see also Mark 6:17–27). Luke has already narrated Jesus' own baptism by John and John's proclamation that Jesus was the promised Messiah, but Jesus' way of being the Messiah is not what John expected. As a prisoner, when would he be set free? To quote Jesus' own words, 'He has sent me to proclaim release to the captives' (4:18).

John sends some of his followers to find out who Jesus really is. In reply, Jesus tells them to report back to John all that they are witnessing. Look and listen: the blind see, the lame walk and the lepers are healed (v. 22). Added to all the healings are the displays of abundant love and extravagant generosity that we read about in chapter 6. John himself had preached solidarity, generosity and endurance (3:10–14), but not to the extreme to which Jesus takes these.

If Jesus were to answer the messengers' questions directly with, 'Yes, I am the Messiah,' he might end up in prison immediately. Instead, he challenges the crowd which has witnessed his interaction with John's friends. There is a question behind the question, 'What did you go… to look at?' (v. 24). It is, 'What are your expectations of a prophet or a king?' If the people were expecting a king like Herod or the Roman emperor, they will not find him in Jesus. Luke powerfully narrates the judgement on those who insist on holding on to their expectations and do not accept the invitation to journey with God in this new reign: 'The Pharisees and the experts in the law, not having been baptised by him, rejected God's purpose for themselves' (v. 30). Those who are least, the rejected and outcast, are the wise ones who accept the invitation to journey with Jesus.

3 Important women

Luke's ability as a storyteller is brilliantly displayed in this narrative of the sinful woman who cannot stop kissing Jesus' feet and anoints them with expensive perfume. One can almost feel the awkwardness of the scene, hear the woman's crying and smell the oil. It is not hard to imagine how distinctly uncomfortable this event was to Jesus' host, Simon the Pharisee, or to see the other guests looking at each other with expressions of horror and embarrassment.

Through the actions of the woman and the dialogue between Jesus and Simon, Luke highlights the full meaning and implications of the good news that Jesus brings. Luke also reminds his readers once more of all the people to whom Jesus extends the invitation to follow him. Jesus himself has accepted Simon's invitation to have dinner at his home (v. 36). One can imagine a modest building, perhaps with an open courtyard where servants bring food to those reclining at the table. It is a hot and dusty Middle Eastern evening. The dinner guests are interrupted by a woman whose reputation is questionable, who proceeds to cry profusely and to touch the feet of the guest of honour with her hands and her hair. Awkward indeed!

But Jesus sees the woman's actions as an expression of her faith (v. 50). Though we are not told explicitly that Jesus extended an invitation to her, it is clear from the text that, like Peter and Levi, she has accepted the call to follow. This is the good news of the kingdom – God's grace and forgiveness extend to all, no matter how great or small their sins. The point of verse 47, 'the one to whom little is forgiven loves little', is not that we should sin more in order to appreciate God's grace more deeply. Rather, Jesus wants to remove the blinders that keep us at arms' length from God's love; he wants Simon (and us!) to love him as extravagantly as the woman does. His is the power of God to forgive all sins (v. 49).

Jesus and his disciples continue their journey proclaiming the gospel of God's reign (8:1). Just as the sinful woman had generously washed Jesus' feet, Luke tells us that other women, Jews and Gentiles, also provided for Jesus and the twelve. Scandalously, they had also left everything to follow him – together, they are signs of the new era.

4 Stories that transform

The theme of journeying comes up again in this famous parable of the sower, but this time we hear of the ways the seed of the word of God falls on roads, in bushes or on rocks. The crowds who have gathered around the celebrity Jesus have been on their own journeys, coming from all over the region to hear him teach (v. 4). Presumably they have witnessed some of the healings or even heard rumours of the scandalous woman who wiped Jesus' feet with her hair and the odd group of fishermen, tax collectors and women who travelled with him.

As Tom Wright points out, we have seen examples of the seeds in this parable in previous narratives: the Jews in Nazareth who heard the word and refused to accept it are like the seed trampled underfoot; Simon the Pharisee, who invites Jesus to dinner but then witnesses his behaviour towards the woman, is like the seed that lands 'among the stones of his prejudice, and nothing can get near it to nurture it and allow it to grow' (Wright, p. 94); the people whose expectations of the kingdom are not met by John or Jesus are the seed choked by thorns; and the centurion, the tax collector and the women, those who accepted the invitation to follow, are the seed on good soil – their faith produces fruit.

In different ways, all the gospels portray the disciples as rather slow learners. Perhaps Luke inserts this explanation of the parable to the twelve with a hint of irony, as he places it soon before they wonder about who Jesus is (8:25). Jesus knows their journey of faith is one that will require patience and endurance (v. 15). Luke and the Christians to whom he writes have heard of the path the disciples had been on and the dangerous fate that came to many of them. Indeed, they did produce fruit – the seed of the word of God and the good news of Jesus' kingdom was spreading throughout the world.

In God's new era, nothing will be hidden (v. 17). The light of justice and love exposes the injustice and oppression of this world, revealing to those who have eyes to see and ears to hear the extravagant generosity and compassion of God.

41

5 Redefining family

The new rules of engagement for this journey with Jesus not only disrupted religious, social or economic norms and conventions, but also challenged the boundaries of family ties and where one places one's true allegiance. Jesus' comment about his family seems harsh to modern ears, even dismissive. It would have sounded even more shocking to those around him because of the very high importance their culture placed on family and heritage. Did Jesus not care that he was descended from the long and noble line of Abraham, Jacob and David, as Luke stresses in the genealogy?

It would be a huge mistake to read this text as an excuse to neglect one's family or to think Jesus did not love and pray for his family. Rather, the point Luke makes is closely tied with the previous text about the word of God that takes root in a person's life and produces fruit. The new community that Jesus was gathering around himself was shaped and held together by God's word. This is not a dismissal of his birth family, but an inclusion of all those who might have been excluded, who now are welcomed because of their practice of faith and trust in God.

To join Jesus on the journey, to be part of this new family, one must learn to trust and to bear witness to the power of Christ. A person who bears good fruit is the one who is rooted in the good soil and introduces Jesus to others through their words, deeds and character. The next two stories highlight these points.

First, we witness the fearful and doubtful disciples, who show no trust in the one who is with them in the boat. Initially, they are more afraid of death than they are of the Master (v. 24), but after Jesus rebukes the storm, they learn a little about faith and about fearing God more than death (v. 25).

Second, Luke paints again a vivid image within the context of the healing of the demoniac man. You can almost hear the squealing pigs, the shouts of the possessed man and the clanking chains that tried to hold him still. Jesus' power is such that even a legion of demons shrinks to nothingness before him. Jesus himself clears the thorns and rocks that might have killed the seed and places the man in good soil, so that he now tells everyone about Jesus. The man freed from demons, the disciples, women, Gentiles – this is the new family.

6 Interrupted by grace

The people in the country of the Gerasenes asked Jesus to leave after they saw what he had done to the demoniac man and the pigs (8:35–37). In contrast, when Jesus returns to Capernaum he is welcomed by the crowds as is fitting for a local celebrity (v. 40). One who is eagerly waiting for him is a leader in the synagogue, Jairus. Perhaps he witnessed Jesus' healing of the centurion's slave just a few days before. Since his only daughter is near death (v. 42), he knows Jesus is his last hope. Unlike the centurion, who did not think he was worthy for Jesus to enter his home (perhaps because he was a Gentile; see 7:6), Jairus begs Jesus to come quickly to his house to heal his child (v. 41).

Just as Jesus answered the centurion's request, so he goes to Jairus' house, but there are crowds pressing in and there are delays. The scene is not unlike an ambulance getting stuck in traffic today. Then Jesus is interrupted by a woman who has been suffering from haemorrhaging for exactly as long as Jairus' daughter has been alive: twelve years. Luke highlights not only her illness but also her economic situation – she has nothing left because she has spent all she had searching for a cure (v. 43).

Wherever Jesus went, healing power went out from him (compare 6:19). The woman touches his cloak to receive such healing and, though she tries to hide, Jesus notices. Both the woman and Jairus have the same behaviour when in Jesus' presence – they fall before him (vv. 41, 47). The woman is healed because of her faith (v. 48), and at that same moment Jairus gets the news that his daughter has died. Jesus goes to the house, holds the dead girl by the hand and raises her to life (v. 54).

Part of the rules for journeying with Jesus include transgressing boundaries. In these healing stories Jesus is touched by the woman (v. 44), then he holds the hand of a corpse (v. 54) – both taboos in that culture. Yet as we have seen all along, the reign of Christ is one for life, not death. Preparing his disciples (and us) for that kind of life is the subject of the rest of Luke's gospel, right up to the resurrection, and then on to Acts and how life is lived in God's kingdom.

Guidelines

- We live in a culture that is often hesitant at best, and more often cynical, about stories of miraculous healings. In Luke's gospel, Jesus' power and authority as the true Messiah are intimately connected with his healing powers. How are we challenged by these sacred texts to rethink our prejudices and scepticisms about the power of God? Could it be that, like the disciples in the boat, we are still more fearful of death than we are of God?

- Jesus creates spaces and places around his own body where strangers and even enemies come together. With Jesus, they are brought into a new family that is shaped by obedience to the rules of God's kingdom. As we grow closer to Jesus, we will grow closer to one another, even to people we do not like. How can we learn together to see others with the eyes of Jesus and to learn to live as witnesses of this new, revolutionary kingdom?

FURTHER READING

Judith Lieu, *The Gospel of Luke (Epworth Commentaries)* (Epworth, 1997).

James Woodward, Paula Gooder and Mark Pryce, *Journeying with Luke: Lectionary Year C* (SPCK, 2012).

Tom Wright, *Luke for Everyone* (SPCK, 2001).

The Bible and disability

Rachel Tranter

'Disability' is a hugely broad term, encompassing physical and cognitive impairments of all kinds. Each person's experience of disability is so unique that there is little commonality, even among those with the same disability. Undoubtedly, the Bible has been used, in the past and in the present, to further marginalise and alienate people with disabilities, particularly in the language of 'perfection' used throughout scripture and in the framing of disabilities as a judgement on sin.

In these notes we will focus on people with physical disabilities, partly because I have a physical disability myself and partly because there is not space in a single week to cover cognitive disabilities as well. I have severe scoliosis, which has given me two 60-degree curves in my spine. Although this causes me pain and discomfort, it is not apparent to most people, and as a result I am not visibly disabled. I (along with many, many other people) exist in the strange space between 'disabled' and 'able-bodied'.

My approach to disability in the Bible is redemptionist; that is, I believe that the passages we will look at can be redeemed from their previous interpretations that have favoured able-bodied people and disadvantaged those with disabilities. At the same time, we must always be mindful not to read our own interpretations into biblical texts. I hope these notes cause you to look at the Bible with fresh eyes, and that they will give you a renewed appreciation for the redemptive work of God for all people.

Bible quotations are taken from the NRSV.

1 The priestly code

Leviticus 21:16–24

In Leviticus 21:16–24, priests who have a 'blemish' are prohibited from serving food at the altar: 'No one of your offspring throughout their generations who has a blemish may approach to offer the food of his God' (v. 17). Interestingly, one of the prohibitions is against anyone who is 'a hunchback' (v. 20); this presumably includes those with scoliosis, such as me. This list includes mainly external defects, which suggests that this is an aesthetic prohibition rather than a practical one. It is possible to conclude from this prohibition that the priests represent the perfection of God. This of course leads to the ableist reading that, if God is without defect, then anything (or anyone) with a defect is considered unholy or a desecration.

However, note that people with these specific disabilities are only excluded from the Holy of Holies and from sacrificing at the altar; they are still permitted to complete other priestly functions and to eat the sacrificial meal (v. 22). If we look wider into the Levitical narrative, we discover that not even unblemished priests are fully 'abled' when it comes to serving in the temple (Leviticus 8); the bodies of priests must undergo ritual washing and covering: 'they must be made "able" by ritual action' (Melcher at al., pp. 81–83). Furthermore, priests with disabilities are also not considered ritually impure, because they are still permitted to eat the consecrated bread.

Even though no one can be 'perfect' in the way that God is said to be, it can still be problematic for people with disabilities to hear of the 'perfection' of God, or indeed of Christ being the unblemished sacrifice for our redemption. For now, perhaps, we must admit that the answer cannot be found in this passage alone and needs to be considered in the light of the whole narrative of scripture. We need look no further than Leviticus 19:14 for the command: 'You shall not revile the deaf or put a stumbling block before the blind.' For now, we must hold in tension the idea of God as unblemished and undefiled alongside Christ as having an impaired and disabled body, to which we will return.

2 Mephibosheth

Mephibosheth is a character with a physical disability: he has been 'crippled in his feet' since he was young (4:4). To some extent, Mephibosheth's disability serves as evidence of the lack of future for Saul's line; the reader would be reassured that Mephibosheth's disability precludes him from ever being a threat to David's throne.

In 2 Samuel 9, Mephibosheth is invited to stay at the Jerusalem court by David, following the latter's promise to Mephibosheth's father Jonathan. Here, it seems we are to pity Mephibosheth. Many commentators interpret David's kindness towards Mephibosheth as representing the *hesed*, loving-kindness, of God towards his people, and perhaps even see David as a representative of divine grace. Some have suggested that David should be applauded all the more for bringing not only a relative of his enemy but a *disabled man* to his table. This degrades the character of Mephibosheth and ends up making the narrative all about David (the able-bodied, handsome man) instead of a more liberating interpretation which might see Mephibosheth's agency and the importance of his inclusion at all in Israel's history.

However, the character of Mephibosheth is not defined entirely by his disability. He has numerous appearances in scripture (he appears in 2 Samuel 4:4; 9:1–13; 19:24–30 and is mentioned in 16:1–4; 21:7), showing how people with disabilities can fully participate in the story of God's people. Furthermore, Mephibosheth does not fit the stereotype of a person with disabilities; he is given agency and independence in making his way to Jerusalem to meet with David. In addition, it is likely that David had ulterior motives (or at least mixed motives) in bringing Mephibosheth to the Jerusalem court, essentially keeping him a hostage. This interpretation makes the able-bodied David less of a hero and instead gives a more nuanced picture of the narrative oppositions between disability and ability.

Mephibosheth appears for the final time in 2 Samuel 19, after David has defeated the uprising led by his son Absalom. Here, his disability is hardly in view. This time, it is David who is coming to Jerusalem; the agency of the one who must do the travelling to the capital has been reversed. Crucially, in the dispute between Ziba and Mephibosheth, which David solves by giving half the land to each, it is Mephibosheth who has the final word, unlike 2 Samuel 9, which is bookended by Ziba talking with David.

3 Job

Job is a prosperous man whose fortunes are suddenly reversed when his children are killed, his businesses ruined and his body struck down with a skin disease. Although the book never uses an equivalent term for 'disability', Job's disease significantly impairs his everyday life and his plight mirrors the experiences of many with disabilities.

Even though Job is determined that no fault of his has contributed to his condition, it's easy to be sympathetic to the view of Job's friends, Eliphaz, Bildad and Zophar, that sin causes suffering. The whole reason Job is outraged at his suffering is that he *hasn't* sinned, suggesting that if he *had*, his misfortune would have made sense and been justified. This can lead to the interpretation that the person with a disability is responsible for their own condition. Furthermore, it is difficult to escape the interpretation that God caused (or at least allowed) this disease to afflict Job. God never answers these charges in the final speech, so we (and Job) never receive an answer about why this is.

A liberating disability reading of the book of Job must wrestle with these ideas. There are two interpretations that are particularly worth mentioning. First, Job identifies himself with the monsters Leviathan and Behemoth, in that they are both attacked by the divine: 'Am I the Sea or the Dragon that you set a guard over me?' (7:12). However, in the divine speeches at the end of the book, Leviathan and Behemoth are shown as marvels of God's creation. Instead of being chaotic monsters, they are shown to be magnificent (Job 39—40). When these passages are mapped on to the metaphor of disability, we can see how Job's disgust with his body does not translate to God's disgust. As is clear from the wider biblical narrative (e.g. Genesis 1; Psalm 139:14), Job's body is part of creation's magnificence: created, affirmed and loved by God.

Second, and surprisingly overlooked, is the fact that the epilogue of the book never states that Job's skin disease is healed. While Job gets a new family and a new fortune to replace those he lost, the text is quiet about his disability being healed. This is especially significant given the number of times Job's friends attempt to link his skin disease with sin. Therefore we must reject the interpretation that disability is a result of divine punishment or that wholeness means being able-bodied. Job can be blessed, whole *and* disabled at the end of his story.

4 Jesus' healings

Jesus' ministry was marked by his miraculous healings, and many of these were performed for people we would now say had disabilities. The healing narratives fit into two broad categories: ones with a Christological emphasis, in which the focus is on Jesus and his actions and where the person with disabilities is often nameless, voiceless and passive (e.g. Luke 14:1–4); and ones with an emphasis on faithful discipleship, in which the person who used to have a disability becomes a paradigm of faithfulness (e.g. Luke 5:25). We can immediately see why the former narratives are not liberating, as there is a lack of agency. The latter have also been used to prove the moral imperfection of people with disabilities, or even to see their lack of healing as something for which they alone are responsible.

The healing stories also have the implication that to become part of the church community, one must be healed of disabilities first. This allows some commentators to suggest that it would have been impossible for Jesus to have had close disciples with disabilities, because he would have immediately healed them. Similarly, while we can praise the healing narratives for showing the cured characters being reintegrated into the community, this fails to consider that, by extension, those who were never healed in the first place are still excluded. When these stories are read today, they can leave people with physical disabilities feeling alienated and excluded. While these healings may be representative of God's saving plan for everyone, it is still difficult to get away from the fact that the stories of Jesus' healings have contributed to the marginalisation of those with disabilities, rather than their inclusion.

The story of the man born blind in John 9 arguably has the best example of the agency and personality of the person healed, but it is not entirely satisfactory. Though the man ends up being a witness to Jesus and likely becoming a disciple, he only reveals God's works, as Jesus predicts (v. 3), *after* having been healed. However, the fact remains that Jesus consistently treated those he met with compassion and inclusion; indeed, in the Nazareth manifesto (Luke 4) it is clear that people with disabilities are at the very heart of Jesus' ministry. Perhaps this example of inclusion is the liberating message that the people of God must imitate.

5 Jesus as disabled

The interpretation of Jesus as disabled was pioneered by Nancy Eiesland in *The Disabled God*. She argues that Christ can be seen as disabled through two aspects of his being. The first is that Jesus' body is metaphorically broken every time we participate in the Eucharist. The second is that, post-resurrection, Jesus embodies impaired hands, feet and side alongside the very image of God. Isaiah 53:3 reminds us that Jesus is 'acquainted with infirmity'. Indeed, Jesus' passion certainly saw him experience weakness and exclusion, allowing him to fully enter into the experiences of many people with disabilities. So, clearly there is a link between suffering and disability, in which Jesus participates.

Eiesland goes on to describe a vision she had, in which she saw God sitting in a wheelchair. While this is clearly Eiesland's personal experience, which she is not claiming as a universal view of God, she is challenging the symbols that Christians use to represent God. Instead of emphasising themes such as 'sin and disability, virtuous suffering, and segregationist charity' (p. 93), we should instead look for empowering and liberating symbols that change people's view of and relationship with God, for both people with disabilities and able-bodied people.

One such symbol is used in the Bible itself: that of Jesus as the 'Lamb standing as if it had been slaughtered' (Revelation 5:6). This vision of Jesus as injured, passive and weak is extremely far removed from the idea of power and invulnerability that is often associated with God. For many, seeing God as the slaughtered lamb or God in a wheelchair is completely different from the 'super-abled' God that we might interpret from passages such as 'The Lord's hand is not too short to save, nor his ear too dull to hear' (Isaiah 59:1) or 'It was fitting that God... should make the pioneer of their salvation perfect' (Hebrews 2:10a).

While the image of God as disabled will remain unpalatable for some, we must still overcome those interpretations that portray God as physically strong in human terms. Indeed, the Hebrews verse ends with 'perfect *through sufferings*' (Hebrews 2:10b, italics mine). Our God is not an unblemished God.

6 The new heaven

God's vision for the whole of humanity comes to its climax in Revelation 21:4 with the description of the new heaven and the new earth. This has been interpreted through an able-bodied lens to argue that heaven will be paradise because it will be free from disability. However, interpreting the lack of 'mourning' and 'pain' in this way presupposes not only that disabilities cause these things but also that they are symptoms of humanity's sin, which need to be removed in order for there to be perfection. As we have seen, it is not liberating to be told that you are included only if you change; many people with disabilities see them as part of their identity, and these sorts of interpretations have led them to believe that their identities will be erased with their resurrection bodies.

A more liberating interpretation of Revelation 21 must neither exclude nor erase people with disabilities. Instead of seeing God as 'super-abled', something that is difficult to maintain in view of the slaughtered lamb representing both ultimate power (being unblemished) and ultimate vulnerability (being blemished), we can note that Jesus bears the scars of his crucifixion in his resurrected body; in fact, these scars were one of the things which caused the disciples to recognise Jesus in his resurrected body. Early Christian theologians interpreted this as meaning that our own resurrected bodies would not be free from disabilities and scars.

Furthermore, and perhaps more importantly, it is not only people with disabilities who will be transformed in the new heaven; we are all in need of transformation and no one will look 'normal' in the way that we understand it in this world. Perhaps the new heaven will be a place which overcomes all of our present society's disabling aspects – although we must take caution with this view, as it may lead to picking and choosing which disabilities constitute 'suffering' and which do not. For many disabilities, including my own which causes me daily pain, no amount of accessibility can fully solve the impairments they cause. However, what is truly liberating is to know that whatever the physical reality in the new heaven, the resurrected, spiritual bodies of both able-bodied people and people with disabilities will be redeemed and transfigured to God's glory.

Guidelines

I hope that these notes have been illuminating and allowed you to look at scripture in a new light. While we can see liberating results through redeeming passages from their previous interpretations, I say again that we must always be careful not to read our own interpretations into the text. Having said that, however, we get ableist interpretations from scripture because we live in a world where able-bodied bias is pervasive. Resisting these common (and often historical) interpretations is imperative if people with physical disabilities are to feel seen and respected.

Ultimately, every human being needs liberation. Even the healthiest of us is only temporarily able-bodied, and we all need transformation. We all need to be saved from our discrimination and bias. It is certainly liberating for people with physical disabilities to know that, in the context of eternal salvation, we are no more 'imperfect' or 'weak' than anyone else.

You may like to ponder the following questions:

- Do church leaders in modern times need to be physically 'unblemished' in order to lead? What (if anything) might exclude them?
- Mephibosheth is one of the few named characters in scripture who have a physical disability, but his story is rarely talked about, even in the field of disability studies. How can you amplify and promote the voices and stories of people with disabilities?
- It goes without saying that not all people with disabilities will be healed (or indeed will want to be healed). How can your church be a space that acknowledges and embraces this?
- How much of your identity is tied up in your body being able to do all the things you can do now? Can you see yourself as simply 'temporarily able-bodied'?
- Have you ever thought about God or Jesus as being disabled? Does this make you uncomfortable? If so, sit with these feelings and bring them to God. What might he want to tell you about your attitude towards people with disabilities?
- What does 'paradise' look like to you? Does it exclude people with disabilities? How might you start changing your approach to this?

FURTHER READING

Hector Avalos, Sarah Melcher and Jeremy Schipper (eds), *This Abled Body: Rethinking disabilities in biblical studies* (Society of Biblical Literature, 2007).

Brian Brock, *Disability: Living into the diversity of Christ's body* (Baker Academic, 2021).

Deborah Creamer, *Disability and Christian Theology: Embodied limits and constructive possibilities* (Oxford University Press, 2009).

Nancy Eiesland, *The Disabled God: Toward a liberatory theology of disability* (Abingdon Press, 1994).

Roy McCloughry, *The Enabled Life: Christianity in a disabling world* (SPCK, 2013).

Sarah Melcher, Mikeal Parsons and Amos Yong (eds), *The Bible and Disability: A commentary* (Baylor University Press, 2017).

Amos Yong, *The Bible, Disability, and the Church: A new vision of the people of God* (Eerdmans, 2011).

Psalms Book IV (Psalms 90—106): the true king restored

Bill Goodman

Previously in this series, we have seen the thought and care in how the psalms have been arranged in their five books, highlighted under the following headings:

- Book I (Psalms 1—41): David's prayers and teaching
- Book II (Psalms 42—72): prayers of David and others – God's message for the world
- Book III (Psalms 73—89): David's inheritance devastated – prayers after kings have failed

Entering the Psalter through the crafted gateway of the first two psalms, we found glimpses of David's struggles and eventual rise to power as king, followed in Book II by hopes that David's God might be acknowledged more fully by Israel and more widely by other nations. But then, in Book III, we encountered crushing disappointment, with foreign enemies overrunning both Israel and Judah. This book ended in crisis, with the question: has God now given up on his covenant with David (Psalm 89:49–51)?

In Book IV, that focus on David virtually disappears. Instead, we encounter Moses, mentioned seven times, from the very first words (the title of Psalm 90) to the closing psalm (Psalm 106). Book IV reminds us of a longer-term perspective: since ancient times, long before human kings appeared, Yhwh God has been this people's true king. That divine rule continues now and always will do, even when those people are crushed and some are in exile.

The content and shape of the Psalter were probably finalised by Jewish exiles permitted to leave Babylon. Returning to their promised homeland and rebuilding their temple brought joy and hope. But that new temple was less grand than the former one and life was full of challenges – and self-rule under the line of Davidic kings was not restored. These disappointments prompted a sense of 'exile' as a continuing experience, still relevant to their ongoing situation.

Bible quotations are taken from the NIV or are the author's own translation.

1 Counting each day, making each day count

Psalm 90

A crisis can be jolting and prompt us to reflect – to step back, to see how we got there and glimpse possibilities for the future. Psalm 90 suggests that kind of experience. Defeat and forced exile at the hands of the Babylonians prompts a searching rethink: what can the past teach? What might the future hold?

The opening words (in the heading) point us not to King David but much further back, to 'Moses the man of God'. It was Moses who brought God's saving power to the tribes of Israel and led them from despair to hope. Psalm 90 goes on to echo the words Moses used when praying for his people in their moment of failure (Exodus 32:11–13). It was Moses who proclaimed the eternal kingship of God (Exodus 15:18), a truth which will become central to this book of the Psalter. And long before even Moses, it was this majestic God who existed, ruled and created (v. 2).

Psalm 90 declares: 'Lord, *you* have been our dwelling-place throughout all generations' (v. 1). Previously the Jerusalem temple's holy sanctuary was declared to be God's dwelling place (Psalm 76:2; also 84:4). But now, with that temple destroyed, the focus shifts to God in person: true pilgrim worshippers need to come to Yhwh. This sets the tone for the psalms that follow (91:9, for example).

Throughout Psalm 90 we find poignant reminders of the passing of time and the transient brevity of life. This might seem gloomy, until the turning point in verse 12. The key to wisdom is to 'number our days'. However much or little time we have on earth needs to be received as a gift: acknowledging that we will eventually die, let us then make each day count. Those who do this can experience the passage of time as something positive rather than disappointing. Satisfaction, even joy and gladness, become possible (vv. 14–15), as we experience God's faithful love and make the most of each day, while entrusting our lives and future to God.

In all this, people need to respond to God's call, turning back to Yhwh (v. 3) and crying out to this compassionate God to turn back to them (v. 13). Then, as they draw on the Lord's strength, the task of rebuilding broken lives and a broken world can begin (v. 17).

2 Taking refuge, finding protection

Psalm 91

Echoes can be evocative, unexpected, bringing us up short. Sometimes particular words or images in one psalm provide a link, echoing the previous ones. Psalm 90 asked God to 'satisfy us' and let 'your deeds be shown' (90:14, 16); now God answers that request, promising to 'satisfy' those who trust him and 'show' them salvation (v. 16). In the closing agonies of Book III, Yhwh was accused of 'hiding' from those who cried out to him (88:14; 89:46); now we find a startling reversal of that image – far from hiding away, Yhwh is truly available as a 'hiding place' for those who trust him (v. 1). The key thing is for them to dwell with God and take refuge in him, to be pilgrims who rest secure in the shelter God gives (vv. 1–2).

A stream of breathtaking promises flows forth, declaring safety at home and safety when travelling. Mention of plagues, surviving impossible odds and angelic bodyguards reminds us of the Exodus account of the Israelites escaping from Egypt. The voice speaks with the assurance of one who has found all this true in personal experience.

Then suddenly, in the closing verses, the voice changes: we hear God responding in person to the passion and trust of the earlier speaker (vv. 14–16). A further stream of promises affirms emphatically that God will deliver, set on high, answer, be with, rescue, honour, satisfy and show salvation to this one who so loves and desires God.

After the previous three psalms, this one can seem ridiculously naive in its beautiful promises and assurance. Little wonder that it has been found written on jewellery used as a magic charm against demons, or worn on dangerous journeys and in pandemics. It promises protection, guarantees safety – to one who trusts deeply in God, who knows and loves God (vv. 1, 14). Yet the fact that Satan quotes this psalm when tempting Jesus (Matthew 4:6) is a warning that it can be misused; it does not invite us to run into danger or put God to the test. Other voices which we have already heard in the Psalter testify that the faithful are not always protected from suffering (as Hebrews 11:35–38 also testifies). All these diverse testimonies are held together and presented to us in the Psalms.

3 Sabbath refreshment brings strength and fruitfulness

Psalm 92

Did worshippers in the Jerusalem temple find trees there? The interior was certainly lined with fine wood and embellished with images of date palm trees (1 Kings 6:15, 29, 31). Today's psalm takes up the image of the righteous person as a tree, which we saw at the opening of the Psalter (1:3); that tree was planted by streams, whereas here we glimpse trees planted in the temple courtyards (vv. 12–13). Perhaps this imagery hints that there were literal trees there, shading human worshippers, providing reminders of the garden of Eden and the goodness of creation (see also 52:8). We cannot say for sure.

This psalm has a unique title: 'Song for/of the sabbath'. This suggests a lens through which to read it. On the sabbath, the faithful cease the works of their own hands and take time to delight in the works of God's hands (vv. 4–5; compare 90:17). The sabbath is a day to deepen one's understanding of Yhwh's faithful love and to declare it, in worship and testimony, joyfully singing out with a variety of musical accompaniment (vv. 1–5). Like the speaker we met in Psalm 73, these worshippers find assurance in the face of life's threats and injustice, as their perspective is restored through focusing on Yhwh (vv. 7–11). Refreshed through worship, they express a hopeful determination to continue being fruitful for God, even in older age (vv. 14–15).

In Book III of the Psalms, we heard voices grieving at the destruction of the Jerusalem temple. Book IV seems to reflect what followed, the exile in Babylon. Psalm 92 may be a reminder of what has been lost: worship in the temple is no longer possible. Yet its presence here also affirms that worship continues, just as the sabbath continues, no matter what circumstances and situations God's people find themselves in.

Life's challenges have not gone away; enemies and evil still seem formidable; but Yhwh is still on high, and still lifting up the faithful ones who battle on (vv. 7–11). Psalm 89 asked whether God's steadfast love and faithfulness had gone missing; this psalm affirms and rejoices that they are still to be experienced in this latest season of life (v. 2). They are what enable worshippers to stand tall, like strong cedar trees and fruitful date palms (v. 12).

4 Chaos, stability and the king's justice

'Yhwh reigns / has become king!' This opening declaration will reappear in the psalms that follow (Psalms 93—99), providing the theological centre of Book IV of the Psalter. We heard similar themes earlier, in Psalm 47, for example. But the emphasis on God showing divine rule in Israel's history now diminishes; Psalm 93 looks back much further, before Israel, even before humanity – to the very beginning of creation. It sees Yhwh asserting kingly authority over the entire world from those earliest moments (compare 90:2).

In the rhythms of 93:3–4, we hear the pounding of rivers, waters and the sea. Is this the sound of hostility or praise? It could be creation giving worship to God (as we shall see in 96:11; 98:7) or, more likely here, the reference is to forces of chaos rebelling against Yhwh's kingly power, seeming to threaten Yhwh's purposes (as in 18:4; 42:7). However, any fears they might raise are brushed aside: God's power is far above all others (93:4; compare 24:1–2; 29:3–4, 10–11). Despite its regular upheavals and turmoil, the world remains secure and stable under God's rule; never again will flood overwhelm it (Genesis 9:11).

In case we are tempted to think that God's kingship means all problems are now sorted out, Psalm 94 brings us back to the everyday world with a jolt – a reminder of the continuing tension between God's promises and present reality. The repeated 'How long?' reminds us of earlier psalms and confirms that the anguish of lament is still experienced (94:3; compare 13:1–2; 89:46). A world in which Yhwh's sovereignty is ignored or despised feels unstable and anxious (94:7, 18–19). Particular Hebrew words connect Psalms 93 and 94: the wicked crush the most vulnerable like the pounding waves that crash on the shore (93:3; 94:5); the exalted divine king must pay back those who exalt themselves (93:1; 94:2).

Psalm 94 presents God as teacher and vindicator, as well as the judge whose justice can be trusted. Along with lament, it exudes confidence that evil will finally be annihilated when God restores the harmony and goodness of creation (94:1–2, 22–23). God's faithful people need to embrace that confidence and live in hope, even as they grapple with the injustices of everyday life.

5 Rejoicing at the king's awesome presence

Psalms 95—96

Sometimes people need the encouragement and challenge of a word of exhortation, particularly when life is hard; those leading the Jewish communities during and after the exile may have sensed such a need. Psalm 95 urges those who hear to 'come' (95:1, 6 – see also 100:4, rounding off this group of psalms). It calls them to exuberant shouts and singing; to heartfelt thankfulness; to reverent bowing down and kneeling; to acknowledge Yhwh as the all-powerful king and creator of all, and as the shepherd of his people. The references to sea and dry land might remind listeners of how God used Moses to lead the Israelites out of slavery in Egypt (95:5; compare Exodus 15:1, 19).

After this upbeat exuberance, the sudden change of mood in the closing verses (95:7c–11) feels bewildering. Now we hear a prophetic voice warning against disobedience and hard-heartedness ('to hear' also means 'to obey' in Hebrew) using an illustration from the time soon after Moses led the Israelites out of Egypt (Exodus 17:1–7). God's holiness has a stern side, presented here in impassioned words about God being angry, even grieving/loathing (95:10–11). Those who proclaim Yhwh's praise must shun rebellion; submission to Yhwh is essential. But like the opening call to worship, this obedience is not forced on anyone: exhortation and invitation call for a free response.

After the sombre, abrupt ending to Psalm 95, the psalm that follows lifts our eyes from human failure to God and what he can do. Once again, the voice exhorts us insistently: to sing (96:1–2), ascribe (96:7–8) and prepare for divine judgement (96:12–13). A new song is needed when God does a new thing: as happened in the past (Exodus 15) and must now happen again. This invitation goes to all the earth, all peoples, all nations – indeed, to all of creation. Let humans realise that they are joined by the oceans, soil, air and trees in glorifying God (compare Psalm 148; also Isaiah 44:23). Let nature and the nations rejoice – including joy at the coming judgement. For divine judgement means the arrival of longed-for justice – a recurring theme in the psalms that will follow (97:2, 8, 10; 98:9; 99:4).

6 Responding to the holiness of the king

Haven't we just been here? Repetition is a feature of this group of psalms (93—100): the opening declaration that 'Yhwh reigns / has become king' (93:1) subsequently reappeared (97:1) and is now proclaimed again (99:1). Alongside these we find two very similar psalms that begin by calling hearers to 'sing a new song to Yhwh' (96 and 98). The divine creator's power over creation, which responds in worship, has been another recurring theme (93:3–4; 95:4–5; 96:11–13; 98:7–9). We can understand why scholars have suggested these psalms might have formed a liturgy for a festival celebrating Yhwh's kingship, complete with procession, singing, blessing and musical accompaniment (95:1–2; 96:1–2; 98:5–6).

Another theme repeated in these psalms is holiness, expressing God's transcendence and 'otherness'. Yhwh dwells in a holy place (96:6) and is to be worshipped in the beauty of holiness (96:9). The righteous give thanks as they remember God's holiness (97:12). Yhwh's right hand and holy arm are what bring salvation (98:1). Now, at the end of this group of psalms, glimpses of divine holiness are drawn together emphatically, in a threefold celebration (99:3, 5, 9).

Echoing Psalm 97, Psalm 99 particularly highlights Yhwh's awesome power and greatness, calling for a response of reverent prostration in worship. Yet it also reminds us that Yhwh does not keep a distance but has chosen to relate to the created world, including humans. Zion is Yhwh's chosen, holy mountain and footstool (99:2, 9) and Jacob is the nation to whom Yhwh has decided to relate (99:4). Great leaders from Israel's past are mentioned – not King David, but priestly and prophetic figures from the more distant past: Samuel, who reluctantly gave Israel their first human king (1 Samuel 8) and Aaron and Moses (99:6–7). Yhwh spoke to his people in the past, bringing justice and forgiveness – and he is still present for this generation as 'our God' (99:8–9).

A right response to all that Yhwh has said and done is summarised in Psalm 100, with its sparkling cascade of exhortations to shout, worship, come, know, enter, thank and praise, addressed not just to 'his people', but to 'all the earth' (100:1). The heart of the matter is to know and acknowledge that Yhwh is God (100:3). This God is a shepherd – an image used of kings (78:71; 80:1; 95:7). Yhwh's goodness, committed love and faithfulness are not just history, but true for each generation (100:5).

Guidelines

- Psalm 90 recommends numbering our days as part of the way to find wisdom (90:12). How will you give thanks for today and make the most of this unique day?

- How do you respond to the promises of protection in Psalm 91? Do they seem ridiculously naive? Do they resonate with your experience – or that of other people you know?

- Reflect on the image of the worshipper as a tree, which we encountered again in Psalm 92. Where do you personally find sabbath refreshment that enables you to become more deeply rooted, more fruitful and able to stand taller? Are you able to find that refreshment regularly?

- Psalms 93—100 proclaim a great confidence in God's rule and coming judgement. What gives us that kind of confidence today – and what can undermine it?

- One of the New Testament writers sensed the relevance of Psalm 95 to a contemporary audience who needed encouragement to persevere in their faith (see Hebrews 3—4). How do you sense this psalm speaking to you? Do those who preach in your church find resources in the psalms, as Hebrews does?

- Some people struggle with the idea of God as 'king', sensing connotations of an overbearing, potentially oppressive, masculine figure. How do you respond to those concerns? As with all the figurative language used in the psalms, in what ways is this picture enriching and what are its limitations?

- A number of these psalms remind us of God's care for all nations and peoples. Keep praying for and learning from those you know in the worldwide church beyond your own shores.

- Glimpses of creation worshipping God also emerge in these psalms. How do you respond to this? Does it change your perception of the hills, fields, forests and soil, the air, rivers and oceans?

1 Leading with integrity

Psalm 101

After being conspicuously absent so far in this fourth part of the Psalter, why does David suddenly reappear in the heading of this psalm? In Psalm 101 we hear the voice of one who is served, has a substantial house and takes responsibility for cutting off the wicked in Yhwh's city; all this suggests a powerful figure such as a king, perhaps speaking at his coronation service or an annual celebration of it. Yet, as we have seen, this fourth book of the Psalms seems to be focused on the time of exile in Babylon, when the line of King David no longer rules in Jerusalem. The focus has shifted to the reign of Yhwh, the true king of Israel (Psalms 93—100).

Whatever the reason for this psalm's heading and its placing here, one of the effects is to suggest hope for a restored monarchy. We briefly glimpse a new David on the throne. This royal figure is in 'the land' and 'the city of Yhwh' (v. 8); in the psalm that follows this one, we find a fuller, rich picture of the restoration of God's people to their land and the restoration of Zion, the place of Israel's temple and focal point of their worship (see 102:13–22). Together these two psalms proclaim a hope that God will come and that God's presence will then endure (102:26–28).

In this new beginning for God's people, the newly restored king demonstrates what it means to walk in the way of integrity (vv. 2, 6), in contrast to the way of the wicked which we noticed at the very beginning of the Psalter (1:1). Details of what that integrity involves emerge, in a mixture of attitudes and actions that could be the code of conduct for this new ruler (vv. 3–8). The headline summary of all this is the call to express both Yhwh's faithful love and Yhwh's justice (vv. 1–2).

When no such ideal new king emerged after the exiles returned from Babylon, hope began to shift to a future Messiah who would truly embody these virtues. The New Testament writers pick up on these hopes as they present Jesus as the true king – and call all his followers to live lives of integrity (John 12:12–15; Colossians 1:9–14).

2 God's abundant grace

Psalm 103

Here is another psalm with the title 'David's' – yet it continues the emphasis we have noticed in Book IV of the Psalter, looking back beyond the reign of King David to the time of Moses. It was through Moses that Yhwh brought justice for his oppressed people in Egypt and continued to act on their behalf after their escape from Egypt (vv. 6–7). Even after they deserted Yhwh to worship a golden calf, restoration came with the wonderful revelation to Moses of God's forgiving grace: the key phrases, found in Exodus 34:6–7, are heard again here and in other psalms (v. 8; compare 86:5, 15; 111:4; 145:8).

God's forgiveness, compassion and covenant are proclaimed and emphasised in this wonderfully rich psalm (vv. 11–14, 17–18). This reminder of God's covenant commitment and forgiveness in Moses' day (and perhaps also in David's day) would give encouragement to people experiencing exile as part of God's judgement. If God's grace was enough to pardon such grievous sins in the past, it suggests hope for exiles in the present and future.

Repetition can be powerful, particularly in such concise poetry. This psalm begins and ends with repeated calls to 'praise' Yhwh, a call to give one's best to the other, perhaps better translated 'worship'. The word 'all' recurs throughout, emphasising the extent of God's claim and God's reach. God is to be 'feared', indicating reverent devotion. Yhwh's mercy and compassion are also repeatedly mentioned (the term used of God's fatherly compassion derives from the word for 'womb', suggesting also a motherly compassion). Perhaps most striking, repeated in this psalm and throughout the Psalter, is the rich word *ḥesed*, conveying Yhwh's faithful, loving commitment (vv. 4, 8, 11, 17).

Those of us from individualistic cultures sometimes need to discover more about being God's people in community. Those from other cultures which have greater awareness of community may need to discover more about the individual's response to God. This psalm affirms the importance of both: it calls us to worship God as individuals (verses 1–5 exhort the self), as human communities (verses 6–18 depict 'all', 'we' and 'us') – and also with the rest of the cosmos, including angelic beings and the whole of God's wider creation (vv. 19–22). Such universal worship is fitting for the one who rules as the true king over all (v. 19).

3 God's creative power and wisdom

Like the previous psalm, Psalm 104 starts and ends with an exhortation to self to worship Yhwh. Psalm 103 ended with an appeal that 'all his works' should worship Yhwh; Psalm 104 portrays the breathtaking diversity and wonder of those works, in a burst of eloquent, exuberant poetry. We sense the breeze and glimpse clouds, sun and moon, oceans and watery springs in mountains and valleys; a profusion of different birds, animals, reptiles, sea creatures, grasses and trees – expressions of God's power and wisdom, all conjured up for us through the skill of the poet.

This celebration of God's creative power echoes the lyrical music of Genesis 1 and Job 38—39. It also offers a counterpoint to Psalm 8, where we noticed, alongside a celebration of the created world, a strong emphasis on the status and responsibilities of human beings as 'royal rulers' on God's behalf. Yet here in Psalm 104, humans are simply glimpsed occasionally alongside the rest of the created world; we see humans as dependent on God (vv. 14–15), habitual workers (v. 23) and sinners who mess things up (v. 35). Psalm 148 does something similar, mentioning humans only briefly among the creatures called to give praise. This puts us in our place, lest we become too full of ourselves and exalt our importance excessively. All creatures – including us – depend on God, who initiates and also sustains life (v. 27).

Like Psalm 8, Psalm 104 seeks to keep us primarily focused not on ourselves or on the wider creation, but on the creator, who is distinct from what is created. An ancient Egyptian hymn with various parallels to Psalm 104 proclaims worship of the sun as the only deity; in Psalm 104 the sun is simply one of God's creations. In some other ancient religions, clouds, wind and fire were a focus of worship; here they too are mentioned as creations, distinct from their creator. We are invited to delight in the created world, but not to fuse or confuse it with the creator, the 'you' or 'he' mentioned throughout as the one who alone is worthy of our worship.

Even the world's chaotic, threatening forces are under Yhwh's control (vv. 25–26). As we noticed in the previous psalm, this awesome God is to be honoured as the majestic king (103:19; v. 1) – yet he also acts as a compassionate parent, nourishing our life as a parent would (vv. 27–28; see 103:13).

4 The story of God's wonderful works

(Read the whole psalm if possible; or else you could omit verses 30–45.)

When seeking to make sense of your life and re-establish your identity, one valuable approach is to retell your own story. Psalms 104—106 provide a poetic reworking of Israel's story, from creation (Psalm 104) through to the time of the Judges. The story is retold selectively and creatively – intending to evoke gratitude and praise. The word 'Hallelu-yah' (an exhortation to 'Praise-Yah', short for Yhwh) makes its first appearance in the Psalter here: it provides the final word in Psalms 104 and 105, then opens and closes Psalm 106, which concludes Book IV. The storytelling reviews the past, but its real interest is in restoring people's sense of purpose and commitment in the present and hope for the future.

Here, as elsewhere in the Bible, we are reminded of the importance of remembering. God's people need to remember who God is and what God has done (v. 5). God also remembers his covenant commitment to his people, which lasts endlessly ('a thousand generations', v. 8) – so even the people's defeat and exile in Babylon has not ended that covenant commitment. The word used for both these rememberings often suggests 'calling to mind', a deliberate and conscious decision to bring things to mind and retain that mindfulness, which then prompts appropriate action.

As with an earlier retelling of the story, in Psalm 78, this one chooses to focus on particular key incidents. In Psalm 105 Yhwh's covenant with Abraham and his sons is emphasised (vv. 6, 9, 42), followed by Yhwh's covenant faithfulness through Joseph and later Moses – all events long before the covenant with David, which is not mentioned. The psalm spends a lot of time reflecting on the imprisonment in Egypt – a topic which would resonate with those who have experienced slavery and exile. Perhaps Yhwh might still be involved in the destiny of enslaved people who feel far from their promised land? Yhwh's gift of the land is also emphasised (v. 11, 44), as is Yhwh's ability to defeat the oppressive superpower of the day (vv. 28–36) – more hopeful hints for the psalm's audience.

The emphasis throughout this psalm is on Yhwh's actions, Yhwh's power and Yhwh's saving grace. Yet the closing verse gives a reminder that such wonderful grace requires a response from Yhwh's people. What will that response be? The story continues in the psalm that follows.

5 The story retold: Israel's response to God's wonderful works

There's more than one way to tell a story. Psalm 106 is a non-identical twin alongside its predecessor, retelling the same story we heard there, the history of God's involvement with Israel, but with a very different slant. Psalm 105's repeated theme is 'We were in trouble, and Yhwh rescued us': it has an upbeat positivity, emphasising God's grace, similar to the historical account in 1—2 Chronicles. Psalm 106, on the other hand, sounds more like 1—2 Kings (and Psalm 78), emphasising the history of Israel's sinfulness and the resulting just punishments.

Both psalms might speak to an audience physically in exile in Babylon, or to a later disillusioned group still feeling 'exiled' despite being back in Judah. The stories about Yhwh's faithfulness to their faithless ancestors are directed at that contemporary audience, deliberately blending the two together using words similar to those ascribed to Solomon (v. 6; compare 1 Kings 8:47). Other biblical writers also do this, mapping the old story on to the current situation. In 1 Chronicles 16 we find an epic song of praise which combines the opening section of Psalm 105 with the closing words of Psalm 106, plus the whole of Psalm 96 sandwiched in the middle. Chronicles was written after the return from exile in Babylon, yet it sets this great song of praise back in the time of King David, as part of the worship in Jerusalem. The story of the beginning of Israel is seen as relevant to successive generations – an approach echoed in the New Testament (e.g. Acts 7; Hebrews 3—4).

This psalm tells what the previous one omitted: the failings of the people of Israel during and after their escape from Egypt. It reminds us of various incidents mentioned in Numbers 11—16, then switches focus to earlier events at Mount Sinai, which we read about in Exodus 32—34. There the covenant relationship was broken by Israel, as they made and worshipped a golden calf, but then restored by Yhwh, through the intercession and obedience of Moses. Here is a hopeful reminder for the psalm's audience that God's covenant commitment to his people continues, despite their rebellion. They may be fickle and unreliable (notice the contrast between verses 12 and 13), but Yhwh remains consistent and faithful.

6 Finding our place in God's story

Psalm 106:24–48

The retelling of Israel's story continues, with the focus shifting to examples which are detailed in Numbers 13—25. The emphasis on Israel's failure continues; the people continued to spurn God's generous provision, grumbling, worshipping false gods, even getting drawn into the horrors of child sacrifice (vv. 24, 36–38). Even Moses proved fallible, lashing out rashly with his mouth when provoked (vv. 32–33).

Yet the key theme remains God's action and faithfulness – expressed in different ways. When the people of Israel were pursued by the Egyptians at the Red Sea, Yhwh simply saved them, despite their lack of faith. In the desert, Yhwh sent trouble on them, but did not destroy them, because of the interventions of Moses and Phinehas. In the promised land and later in exile, Yhwh gave them over to the power of oppressors, but ultimately saved them again through covenant faithfulness.

As in Psalm 105, remembering proves a key issue. Israel's response to Yhwh's saving grace proved disappointing. Psalm 106 unveils a repeated history of unfaithfulness because of failure to remember God's wonderful works (vv. 7, 13, 21–22). This remembering involves knowing the story of God and finding your place in that story – among those who sin, find forgiveness and learn to depend on Yhwh. Those who remember like this discover the wonderful truth that Yhwh also remembers – remembers his covenant (v. 45). So the plea is that Yhwh will continue to remember (v. 4) and save this current generation (v. 47).

This plea is based on an understanding of God's character. God's faithful, loving commitment, distilled into the word ḥesed, which we noticed repeated throughout Psalm 103 and which recurs again here (vv. 1, 7, 45). Alongside that we see God's compassion, which gives hope for a transformed future (vv. 43–46). Grace abounds. So the speaker finds courage to pray that God will gather the remaining exiles back together in their land to worship their God (v. 47). Yhwh, the true king, is still 'our God', whose covenant commitment continues. As in Books I—III of the Psalms, a closing doxology of pure praise (v. 48) is the appropriate response, rounding off this account of history and also this fourth book in the Psalter.

So what does the future hold? What more remains to be said? The fifth and final book awaits us.

Guidelines

- Did one of the psalms we have read from Book IV catch your attention? If so, explore the reasons why. Is there something about it which stands out for you?

- If Psalm 101 can be seen as a code of conduct for a leader of God's people, how does it speak to your church and (if appropriate) to yourself in your roles? What might it say to politicians and business leaders in today's world?

- We noticed various words and ideas repeated throughout Psalm 103. Do any of those stand out for you? If so, make that a focus for your prayer and praise today.

- How does Psalm 104 speak to our current climate emergency and ecological crises? You might reflect on the way it puts us humans in our place, alongside all kinds of other creatures, including wild animals (not just those domesticated for human purposes), valuing them all as Yhwh's possessions (104:17–18, 24). It also depicts powerful forces in the cosmos, which were sometimes seen as the forces of chaos (the sea and Leviathan, 104:25–26), as ultimately under God's control. Does that prompt in us helpful assurance – or unhelpful complacency?

- In Psalms 105 and 106 we noticed the importance of remembering: not haphazardly, but as a deliberate decision to call important truths to mind and keep them in mind. This kind of remembering requires effort and discipline (and is very different from nostalgia). How does the habit of remembering well help us today to identify with those who have gone before us and find our own place in God's story? Is it a habit that needs to be cultivated more in your church's worshipping life?

- Do you ever find a particular psalm feels distant from your own situation – perhaps an angry lament or a serene thanksgiving? If so, you might value John Bell's suggestion: 'When we read the Psalms, our first thought should not be "What does this mean to me?" but rather "For whom has this psalm meaning?" And if it is not me, or if it does not speak about my experience, then let my mind go to those for whom it may well be speaking and allow the psalm to become my prayer in solidarity with them' (*Living with the Psalms*, SPCK, 2020, p. 86).

FURTHER READING

Jerome F. D. Creach, *Discovering the Psalms: Content, interpretation, reception* (SPCK, 2020).

Nancy L. deClaissé-Walford, Rolf A. Jacobson and Beth LaNeel Tanner, *The Book of Psalms (New International Commentary on the Old Testament)* (Eerdmans, 2014).

John Goldingay, *Psalms (Baker Commentary on the Old Testament Wisdom and Psalms)* (Baker Academic, 2005–08; three volumes).

J. Clinton McCann, *Psalms (New Interpreter's Bible, volume 4)* (Abingdon Press, 1996).

Alison Morgan, *World Turned Upside Down: The Psalms and the spirituality of pain* (BRF, 2023).

Frederico G. Villanueva, *Psalms (Asia Bible Commentary)* (Langham Publishing, 2016–22, two volumes).

Mountains of God

John Rackley

Climbing of all sorts is popular today like it has never been before. It speaks to the need to get out there and go beyond your settled self. It is this desire that a theology/spirituality of the mountainside can help nurture into a relationship with God.

In the Hebrew Bible, mountains are often the scenes of great acts of God or important steps of faith for the Hebrew people. Their names resonate through the text and sometimes overlap with each other as the story of God's call to his people develops. Each is a theophany that becomes a deep revelation.

In the New Testament, and the gospel of Matthew in particular, the ministry of Jesus is punctuated by various mountaintop epiphanies. They give shape to his teaching and provide an engagement with the work of God's salvation through him.

In this series, we will consider what the biblical text says about these various mountains and explore how they act as images for our faith journey with the God of the 'high place'. Let us dwell in the mountains of God.

Unless otherwise stated, scripture quotations are taken from the NRSV.

1 Mount Ararat: time for a reset

Genesis 8

The first eleven chapters of Genesis are glorious feats of faithful prehistoric imagination seeking to understand how things have come to be as they are. The story of Noah and the flood describes the ark coming to rest on a mountain that does not exist – Mount Ararat; it was rather in the mountainous *region* of Ararat. The Armenian Church reveres one 5,000-metre peak as the location, and over the years there have been unverified claims that the ark has been found.

Any examination of this account needs to be ready to consider what it says about the nature of God, the development of humankind, the relationship of sacred text to actual events and how the Bible lets the story of God's purposes unfold through conversation and covenant.

Not that Noah says much. God does all the talking. Noah does what God says, showing little initiative until he becomes a vintner, with its ignominious outcome (9:20–23) and his final, somewhat vindictive, words (9:25).

God, on the other hand, seems to have undergone a transformation. Ararat is the Hebrew version of what is believed to be the Assyrian Uartu. It means 'the curse reversed'. The mountain, wherever it might be, is the scene of a deep experience for God the creator. It might be overstating it, but we need to consider that in bringing in the flood, the creator discovered his own devastating power. Yet as he makes a new covenant with all life through Noah, God is withdrawing from his own capacity for violence (8:21).

Here is regret and repentance; Ararat is the scene of a cosmic reset. The violence of humankind needs to be dealt with. Creation is going in a direction that God cannot tolerate. There needs to be judgement passed on sin and evil, but obliteration of the species is not the answer. Here is a hint of grace.

So starts a trend that will come to fruition in Jesus the Son of God – the obedience of the one means the salvation of the many. God responded to the righteousness of Noah, but he was a flawed saint. There will be no more favourites, and rain has fallen on the unjust and just ever since.

2 Mount Moriah: time for testing faith

Genesis 22:1–19

The location of Mount Moriah is commonly taken to be in Jerusalem after a land purchase of David and the building of Solomon's temple (2 Chronicles 3:1–2). But the meaning of Moriah and its location have been disputed from early times, not least by the Samaritans, who locate it near Mount Gerizim, north of Jerusalem (John 4:20).

While the exact location of Mount Moriah is unclear, in the story of Abraham taking his son Isaac to the point of sacrifice, God is clearly watching over events for his own purposes. Abraham is going through a time of testing and God will not be denied.

But what sort of God demands the sacrifice of a favoured child? What sort of man believes that that is the command he must follow? What sort of God or human allows the death of the innocent – be it a boy or an animal?

For some, this is an example of the progressive revelation that we see throughout the Old Testament, where eventually child sacrifice is condemned (Deuteronomy 18:10) and the prophetic tradition belittles animal sacrifice (Micah 6:6–8); a divine revelation which culminated in the sacrifice of grace in the arrival of God's favoured child.

But Moriah is the scene of an intense, mysterious confrontation between belief and trust in the Almighty One. What demands can be expected from the Lord? Moriah is an experience of senselessness. It challenges us not to hide in cosy, easy answers expecting God to sort it all out.

Sometimes we have to climb into a test of faith, where God seems to be only an observer. Since leaving Ur, Abraham had learned that he should not judge the Lord by feeble sense. His journey with his son was yet another walk before the Lord 'not knowing where he was going' (Hebrews 11:8). The Moriah experience insists that we do not evade the awfulness of possible futures when we can trust God is the watchful companion.

Abraham took responsibility for living by faith in a God who expected him to embrace life's impossible dilemmas. He was learning that the journey that God had initiated would always mean he would be a stranger in the unfamiliar territory of God's gracious provision.

3 Mount Horeb: the wilderness experience (1)

Exodus 3:1–17

Moses, a nomadic shepherd, wanders across the desert to a thrilling encounter with God and an experience that reshapes his purpose and direction in life. At the foot of Mount Horeb, which probably means 'a glowing heat', this lonely, disordered exile receives an overwhelming revelation of God. It is the first high place to be called the mountain of God. This makes it both unique and special.

The setting is God's workshop – the wilderness. This is a word which describes not only a landscape devoid of cultivation, apparently barren and lifeless, but also a space beyond the control of civilisation with its conventions and laws, both secular and religious.

It is not necessary to keep mountain and wilderness separate. The mountain arises out of the wilderness. Moses goes to the 'backside of the desert' (v. 1, KJV). Remote, hidden and in the foothills of a mountain, he meets God in the glowing heat of a burning bush.

A key theme here is that of identity. Moses asks of himself, 'Who am I?' (v. 11). He also asks of God (in so many words) who he is (v. 13).

God is the 'God of Abraham, Isaac, and Jacob'. He is also the 'God of your ancestors' (v. 16) and would be known by non-Israelites as the 'God of the Hebrews' (v. 18): a god who breaks into human affairs to 'observe', 'hear', 'know', 'come down', 'deliver' and 'bring out' from slavery; a God who is taking the initiative (vv. 7–8). The encounter with such a God would have been more than enough for Moses to cope with, but God goes further, declaring: 'I am who I am' (v. 14). This is the God of many names and beyond all names: the One who gives everything else meaning.

This is God's challenge to Moses. The experience makes Moses question his ability to cope with God's future for him. Beneath the heights of Horeb, which one day he will get to know well, Moses is given an insight into his true self. Only when this is done can he take on the Egyptian status quo and lead his people towards a time and a place for worship.

Moses travels into a liminal experience of renewal and self-awareness, where desert and mountainside connect, and God is a glowing grace.

4 Mount Sinai: the wilderness experience (2)

Exodus 19:16–23

Today, Jabal Mousa, part of the Upper Sinai Massif, stands for the biblical Mount Sinai. The mountain soars some 2,100 metres above low-lying plains, and imagination can readily see the encampment of Israelite ex-slaves at its foot.

Moses has brought his people to worship at the mountain of God, Horeb, but as often in scripture, a new name emerges. Now it takes its name from the wilderness of Sinai, for there is more than a burning bush there.

There is thunder and lightning, storm and trumpet, cloud and impenetrable darkness. In the midst of this – elusive, hidden yet enticing, unseen but not unheard – is the God Moses first encountered as the God of his ancestors and the God of the Hebrews. But as the story unfolds, his relationship with God undergoes a profound change.

It requires that he climb and keep climbing back up the mountain. His journey begins with God reaffirming the covenant with his people, but it will go beyond that which was made with Noah and Abraham. The word 'beyond' suitably describes the nature of this covenant, for it will arise from the very nature of God.

Moses climbs into the cloud which has come down on the mountain. This cloud both hides and reveals the glory of God. Moses is drawn further into what is beyond the cloud. It is the thick darkness in which God waits (20:21). This is uncomfortable imagery. Culturally for many today, darkness speaks of hurt, evil, shame and what one wants to hide. Yet in this account, Moses shows no anxiety. He wants to see in the dark. His previous experience has given him glimpses of God; now he wants more. God has created in him a thirst for more of what he has only received in part. The darkness of God invites him to go beyond what his senses and intellect can tell him.

God attracts him but also keeps his distance (33:17–23). Moses has come so far, but his longing for God cannot control either events or God. In the dense darkness of God's grace, he will learn that God cannot be tamed by our ideas or beliefs – any more than the wilderness.

5 Mount Nebo: looking into the future

Deuteronomy 34

Mount Sinai is a place to leave, not to stay. The future beckons. There is a journey to be taken through the testing times and hardship of nomadic desert life. Moses has been prepared for it, but it is a difficult experience for the Israelites. But the future is the promised land and, guided by the cloud by day and the fire by night, this hope sustains the journey until there is one last climb for Moses. This time, there is no enticing encounter with God. The path Moses must take has already been decided.

The prophet Moses, the servant of the Lord who has seen God face to face, must now accept his destiny. This final chapter in Deuteronomy is deeply poignant. Moses, under the guidance of God, comes to realise that despite all his achievements, he is only one part of God's plan for his people.

Mount Nebo becomes the place where he can gain perspective on his life. Gaining height, clambering away from the noise of everyday, he can see the direction of travel of God's providence. He looks into the distance and there, across the River Jordan, beyond Jericho, is the land that all his efforts have been about.

Moses accepts responsibility for the way in which the Israelites have turned against God (Numbers 20:12), prepares Joshua to become his successor (v. 9) and accepts that what he has accomplished is all that God has required of him.

From a human perspective, the life of Moses might be considered like an unfinished symphony. But what is incomplete in one time and place may come to completion at another. As Jesus himself would point out on another mountainside, he had come to fulfil the law not to abolish it (Matthew 5:17–18).

So Moses died and 'was gathered to his people' (see Numbers 27:13). This is more than a calming euphemism for death, for the active agent in the life of Moses, as he had been in the lives of Abraham, Isaac and Jacob, was God, the Lord, the 'I am' and the 'I will be'. God gathers up all life, and to die in the will of God is always the gift of life.

6 Mount Zion: transcendent faith

Isaiah 2:1–5

Mount Zion first appears in the Bible as a hilltop fortress captured by King David. It became synonymous with Jerusalem, one of the world's most significant cities. By the time of Isaiah, the temple of Solomon had been built, and its worship and prayer were an expression of profound trust in God.

Yet not all was well. Israel was under constant threat of invasion, and the life and religious activity of the city had become dissolute and self-absorbed. Isaiah is scathing in his attack on Israel's morality and piety, but at the same time he seeks to lift their hearts.

He calls them back to the original covenant of God with Abraham, that through Israel the whole world will be blessed. He offers a vision of the future which transcends their present circumstances. Mount Zion will be at the centre of world affairs. There will be universal desire for faith in the God of Israel. Zion will be a place of deep learning, ushering in an era of perpetual peace. The religious life of Israel, incarnate in the temple, will be the channel of the Lord's teaching. And the end of this will be a world without means of violence or reason for violence – an echo of the covenant made with Noah. This will not be the work of human achievement but of God himself.

This vision of transcendent faith is clearly shared by more than one prophet. Micah 4:4 expands the vision of a non-violent world, stating that 'they shall all sit under their own vines and under their own fig trees, and no one shall make them afraid': an expression of communal harmony that all nations could share.

But who would believe him? No matter how significant in the story of Israel, could Mount Zion have such a future? There was much evidence to the contrary. So Isaiah, using his favourite description of the nation, tells the house of Jacob what they must do in the meantime: 'Let us walk in the light of the Lord!' (v. 5) – a light that had shone through a bush that did not burn and lit up the lightning flashing around Mount Sinai; a light that had once transformed Jacob into Israel and would do so again.

Guidelines

- The story of Noah on Ararat raises questions about what sort of stories are contained in Genesis 1—11. Are they imaginative parables that try to explain the presence of sin and evil in a creation declared good by the creator, or is there more?

- 'Faith cannot evade the awfulness of all possible futures.' How does our faith cope with fear of the unknown?

- How are you aware of the influence of your ancestors on your current way of faith?

- Moses' encounter with the luminous darkness of God on Sinai has inspired many Christian mystics. Do you find this attractive?

- Do you have your own Mount Nebo, where from its height you can get some perspective on what is happening in your life?

- What significance does the vision in Isaiah 2:1–5 have for faith in God today?

1 The mountain of testing

Matthew 4:1–11

Jewish readers would have recognised echoes from their own scriptures in what the Christian writers were producing. This was certainly the case in Matthew's gospel. Mountains feature throughout the text, and while the location of most of them is a matter of conjecture, they all create a composite mountain of divine experience.

Horeb and Sinai are clearly in sight as Matthew describes Jesus' journey in the Judean wilderness: his 40 days of fasting and testing of obedience echo the people of Israel's 40 years of wandering.His time of testing and his baptism are two parts of one experience. He is the new Son of God and, as the people of Israel once did, he must work out the consequences of his vocation. A wilderness can mean a place for those who have been cut off or driven out. This had been the action of the Spirit of God after the baptism (v. 1). It took Jesus beyond the jurisdiction of the religious and political authorities. It was a place for clear thinking, with life reduced to essentials. This is what the Israelites had discovered in their desert wanderings – what would they eat? Could they really trust God? Who was in control?

Jesus responds to each temptation with words from Deuteronomy. Each temptation would have led him to a point of no return. He turns them into an opportunity to demonstrate his devotion to God.

The final test involves a mountain. It provides a world-embracing vista and a none-too-subtle suggestion that would result in false worship. Jesus takes the challenge of Satan head on. There is one God and only that God commands worship (Deuteronomy 6:4, 13).

Matthew describes the site as a 'very high mountain' (v. 8). So is this a reference to Zion, which Isaiah describes as the highest of the mountains? It was certainly in the vicinity of the temple, which had featured in the second temptation. Isaiah asserted that it would be on that mountain that all the nations would receive the teaching of the Lord. Satan claims the means for that to happen. Whatever that might have involved for Jesus, it would mean a distorted vocation and a loss of his identity as the Son of God.

2 The mountain manifesto

The hills behind Capernaum rise gently, are pastoral in nature and are nothing like the harsh mountainsides of Sinai. This would appear to be a self-conscious act by Jesus. Again we are made to think of Moses, the giving of the law and the vocation of Israel. But we should avoid too much dependence on equivalence.

The crowds that gather are drawn from beyond the boundaries of Israel. The quotations from Isaiah emphasise that historically it was the land of the northern tribes. They had been among the first to suffer the darkness of foreign invasion and exile. This was a location where Jew and Gentile still mingled and the fishing industry of Galilee at the time of Jesus served the local Roman colonies.

It is Jesus' healing ministry that draws the crowds, and Matthew succinctly paints the scene. Jesus sees the crowds, goes up the hill with his disciples (only four are named at the time) and, sitting down, begins to teach.

Who is the teaching for? Is this only for the four disciples, with others listening in? Or are the crowds a large gathering of followers from whom the twelve would be drawn (Luke 6:17)? Whoever they were, no one would have been under any illusion as to what Jesus was saying.

The kingdom of heaven (God) was on its way, and life was about to be turned upside down (4:17). Just as at the foot of Horeb God revealed his compassion for the Hebrew slaves and challenged them to think differently about him, Jesus proclaims a similar reversal.

Life in the kingdom would be a surprise, especially for those who benefit from the status quo, like Pharaoh in his time and Herod Antipas in the present. The beatitudes involve a reversal of fortunes, values and perceptions for people. The so-called 'entitled' would no longer have it their own way.

This happy state of blessedness is a divine response to various states of human experience. Their future is bright with hope. Jesus calls the Israel of his day to take up their historic share in the mission of God to bring light to people who live in darkness – not only downtrodden Jews but also the crowds who live beyond Israel's promised land. All is grace. All is gift. All is the generosity of God.

3 The mountain of healing and prayer

Matthew 14:22–23; 15:29–39

Jesus climbs into the hills to pray and to heal. Galilee is a hilly area, and for reasons of peace, quiet and security, Jesus would have used various hillsides.

Much scholarship now accepts that the synoptic gospels are shaped by their relationship with each other, their own sources and the editing of their authors. So far in this series, we have assumed that Matthew is deliberate in the way he introduces the mountain experiences of Jesus, the crowds and the disciples. We cannot ignore this pattern, which becomes more crucial as the gospel story unfolds.

Matthew also constructs his material by significant allusion to the times recorded in the Torah, to help his Jewish listeners recognise Jesus as the new Moses. Like Moses, Jesus goes into a desert place. But more than that, Jesus is also the favoured Son of God. Like God speaking to Moses at the foot of Horeb, Jesus has compassion on the people (14:14; 15:32). He too provides manna from heaven (14:19). What Matthew records is Jesus taking the initiative and interpreting his own calling in terms of the historic vocation of Israel: to be a nation through which all the peoples of the world will be blessed.

In solitary prayer, Jesus speaks to God in the isolation of the mountainside. There is no attempt to turn this into a unique encounter, for the communion between God the Father and God the Son is seamless. Jesus does this regularly. His prayer with God shapes his service of God. In the two miraculous feedings, we are told of particular moments when the transcendent compassion flows through Jesus.

So Jesus brings healing to the crowds as Moses had lifted up the serpent in the wilderness (Numbers 21), and twice Matthew emphasises that it is the mute, the maimed, the lame and the blind who are restored (15:30–31). Thus Jesus fulfils the longing of the exiled Israelites for a creation renewed and restored (Isaiah 35) and a return to Zion. But in Jesus there is more than Zion.

This is an explicit challenge of Jesus. No place, even somewhere as spectacular as the temple, can restrict the action of God.

4 The mountain of transfiguration

Matthew 17:1–9

The inaccessible God shines through the humanity of Jesus as he is transformed before the eyes of his disciples.

The whole account of the transfiguration is shaped by Old Testament allusions: the cloud, the voice of God, the building of desert tabernacles, the shining face of Jesus and the dazzling white of the Ancient of Days (Daniel 7:9). The reader is taken back to Sinai, and it is no surprise then that Moses and Elijah emerge from the shadows of the past as Jesus turns towards Jerusalem to fulfil his purpose. They are both part of the prophetic tradition of Israel, although they are usually described as representing the law and the prophets.

All three (Jesus, Moses and Elijah) are people who lived on the margins and there met God. Both Moses and Elijah had to escape powers that would have destroyed them. Jesus often ministered beyond the villages of Galilee, never went into the local Roman city of Tiberius and attracted people from well beyond the tribal territories of Israel.

The inclusion of Moses and Elijah has been described as a kind of salvation-history summit conference. They have much in common with the disciples. Both prophets and disciples had received a deeper awareness of the presence of God on a mountainside. The prophets, like the disciples of Jesus, saw what was hidden. Their struggles and their faith brought them to a place where the wider picture could be seen.

This is a biblical 'thin place', where eternity breaks through into time and space. It is an experience where humans sense they are being reached by what cannot be seen and are turned towards a new understanding of themselves and their environment.

An encounter with what is always hidden in the mess and matter of life is realised in the one who prays in the rarefied atmosphere of the mountainside. This is an insight that Luke recognises which the other two gospel writers do not include – that their purpose in going up the mountain was to pray (Luke 9:28–29).

The disciples are given an epiphany which they would need to absorb and take time to consider before declaring its significance (2 Peter 1:16–19).

No wonder, then, that Peter is reduced to silence by the voice in the cloud. For after God has spoken, there is nothing more to say but to watch the Son of God descend the mountain and make his exit into further glory.

5 The Mount of Olives

Matthew 24:1–8; Acts 1:6–14

The Mount of Olives dominates both the skyline opposite Mount Zion in Jerusalem and the story of Jesus from his Passion to Pentecost. It has little mention in the Old Testament but has an eschatological significance for Zechariah (14:4). It is the place where Jesus and his disciples speak of the meaning of the future that both he and his followers anticipate involving the temple. It is an appropriate place to discuss ultimate and penultimate times.

It is an 'edge' place. On its eastern slope, the road to Jericho, which Jesus had used in his final journey to Jerusalem, descends swiftly into the desert. Deep in the valley, facing the city, was Gethsemane, where there was a wine press and the grapes began their transformation into fresh wine. To the mount he would return with his disciples after the resurrection. A familiar location for unfamiliar times.

Both in Matthew's account and Luke's, before and after the resurrection, the disciples are still held by a limited eschatology. They can see no further than the reversal of Israel's political and military fortunes. They are still awaiting a messiah who will sweep away the occupation of Rome and restore the dominance of Israel's former power. This was the end game that they believed Jesus would herald, and for them his resurrection is confirmation of this.

These were not the end times that Jesus anticipated. Yet there is no hope of a peaceful descent into a new world. Jesus uses the image of childbirth to describe the approaching events. This is an image powerfully used by three significant prophets: Isaiah, Jeremiah and Micah. His disciples must expect a time of pain and distortion. There is a time of birth approaching, but it will not come without cost.

Out in the desert, Jesus had rejected three different ways of commanding the attention of people, culminating in the mountain-high temptation to rule the world through the schemes of Satan. In the Acts account, he now reminds them of all the times he spoke of the kingdom of God – an experience of God summed up in the 'blessings' first heard on a hillside in northern Galilee. For now, they must turn their back on the desert, for a further revelation of God awaits them in the city.

6 The last mountain

Matthew 28:16–20

A mountain known only to Jesus and his disciples is the scene of his farewell in Matthew's gospel.

We may contrast this with the experience of Moses on Mount Nebo. There, Moses can see the promised land but cannot join his people. They must cross alone under new leadership. He will be honoured but be no more than a memory. Jesus too stays put as the disciples turn to their future, but they will not be alone. He will be with them – the Emmanuel God announced at the beginning of the gospel to Joseph (1:20–23) – a divine presence intimately involved with his people.

We may compare this with his experience in the desert as Satan tempted him with a false promise of world domination. Jesus has the world in view again as he tells the disciples to continue what started among their own people. But they know who to worship, even though some struggle with Satan's temptation.

In his Galilee ministry, Jesus sent them to heal and proclaim the kingdom of God, but not to go to the Gentiles and Samaritans (10:1–8). They were to stick to the areas they knew best and minister to people who would feel they were not strangers. But the resurrection has changed all that. That mission is still theirs to pursue but in new ways and at different times. They are to be Christ's people among people who are not of their background or faith.

For there is a different authority working among them – the worldwide mandate of their risen Lord. No nation or community or culture can now be excluded from his influence and teaching. Discipleship does not stop at the boundaries of the historic people of God.

Unlike the other mountains, there is no descent mentioned – no going down into the plain, no crossing of the wilderness, no journey to a promised land, no return to the city. We are compelled to stay with the timeless command of Christ. There is a disconcerting absence of detail.

Here is an echo of the God who is the 'I am' and the 'I will be who I will be'. This is the God who is more than the God of our ancestors, no matter how much we honour them: the God who will not be contained in any temple or on any mountain.

Guidelines

- Which beatitude makes you most uncomfortable and why?
- What is your experience of praying in isolation and the outdoors?
- Can you recall a 'thin place' experience of your own?
- In John 4, Jesus and the Samaritan woman discuss their respective favoured temple sites. Jesus foresees a time when worship will require no temple (v. 21). What implications – cultural, political and liturgical – do you draw from these words?

God of mountain glory, lift our faith into the heights of your grace and power, so that we long to know and serve you through the One who is with us in all times and places. Amen.

FURTHER READING

Belden C. Lane, *The Solace of Fierce Landscapes: Exploring desert and mountain spirituality* (Oxford University Press, 2007).

Andrew D. Mayes, *Beyond the Edge: Spiritual transitions for adventurous souls* (SPCK, 2013).

Brother Ramon, *The Prayer Mountain* (Canterbury Press, 1998).

Rabbi Jonathan Sacks, *Covenant and Conversation: Genesis, the book of beginnings* (Maggid Books, 2009).

Graham B. Usher, *Place of Enchantment: Meeting God in landscapes* (SPCK, 2012).

Humour in 1 and 2 Kings

Helen Paynter

'Truth and good are not to be laughed at. This is why Christ did not laugh. Laughter foments doubt' – Jorge, in Umberto Eco's *The Name of the Rose*.

Humour? In the Bible? Some readers will share the opinion of Eco's character Jorge. Isn't the very idea of finding humour in scripture scandalous?

Jorge's assertion that Jesus never laughed is hard to sustain, given for example, Jesus' words in Matthew 23:24. 'You strain out a gnat, and swallow a camel.' The crowd would have been amused, though the religious leaders he was addressing would not. But they would have got the point.

Jorge is correct that truth and goodness are not to be laughed at. But humour is sometimes an effective way to uncover the lack of truth or the false appearance of goodness. The magazine *Private Eye* does this very effectively, using humour to expose folly and hypocrisy in the public sphere. Humour need not be frivolous; it can be an important truth-seeking device.

Some who resist the idea of humour in scripture do so because humour is often unkind. And, certainly, the humour we will discover in Kings cannot be accused of kindness. But the Old Testament prophets of old prioritised truth-telling over a veneer of civility. And as we shall see, the humour of scripture is always aimed *upwards* – towards the powerful, the boastful, the hypocritical – never downwards at the weak.

Jorge is also correct that humour tends to foment doubt. But the humour we will uncover never creates doubt about God. It will, however, throw shade on the integrity and wisdom of many characters in the narrative: pagan kings, false prophets – and even God's own servants. For there is no one good – or wise – but God himself.

Unless otherwise indicated, translations are the author's own.

1 Baal's bowels

1 Kings 18:21–40

For many readers, Elijah's great showdown on Mount Carmel is the go-to story if one were to look for humour in scripture. It is widely understood that the prophet sarcastically mocks the 450 prophets of Baal, who are unable to conjure fire: 'Call in a louder voice, for he is a god! Perhaps he is meditating; perhaps he has withdrawn to the side; perhaps he is on a journey; perhaps he is asleep and must be woken' (v. 27).

My translation probably underestimates the intensity of the insult. The precise nature of Elijah's suggestions about Baal's activity is unclear. The second of these verbs only occurs once in scripture, but on etymological grounds it appears to refer to withdrawing to the side, probably to defecate.

As Elijah mocks their god for having a poo, the attempts by the prophets of Baal become frantic. They begin to gash themselves and work themselves up into the sort of prophetic frenzy that is viewed at best ambivalently elsewhere in the Old Testament (compare 1 Samuel 10:5; 18:10). But the louder their cries, the more deafening is the silence of their god: 'But there was no sound and no one answering… But there was no sound and no one answering and no hearing' (vv. 26, 29).

The narrator is brutal as he portrays the pagan prophets fruitlessly attempting to awake their god. He mocks their ritual dance: 'They limped [*pasach*] around the altar they had made' (v. 26). But this is the second time we've encountered the verb *pasach* in this passage. In a different form it was used in verse 21, as Elijah accused the people of vacillation: 'How long will you limp between two crutches? If the Lord is God, go after him, but if Baal, go after him.'

Elijah uses the unflattering language of the prophets' dance to accuse the people of shifting from foot to foot in indecision, as if unevenly shod or hopping between two twigs like an indecisive bird. 'Make up your minds,' he challenges them. 'Which god is worthy of your worship?' I'm reminded of the equally unflattering rebuke of Revelation 3:15–16 (NRSV): 'I wish that you were either cold or hot. So, because you are lukewarm and neither cold nor hot, I am about to spit you out of my mouth.'

Baal may have been on a long toilet break, but half-hearted followers of Yahweh make him puke.

2 Ben-Hadad and Ahab lock horns

1 Kings 20:1–21

The kingdom of Aram, which may be translated 'Syria' in your Bible, was situated to the north-east of the kingdom of Israel, and through the time of the divided kingdom these two nations alternated in their relative dominance. Today we read the first of several encounters between Aram's king, Ben-Hadad, and the king of Israel (here, Ahab; v. 13). Neither king comes out of this story well.

It begins with Ben-Hadad making outrageous demands as he issues a military threat against Samaria, the capital of Israel (v. 1). He sends this message to Ahab, 'Your silver and your gold are mine, and the best of your wives and your sons' (v. 3).

Ahab capitulates instantly (v. 4), hoping to buy off the threat, and it is only at Ben-Hadad's second demand, to search his palace, that Ahab baulks. Is this new reluctance out of concern for his honour (indignation at the suggestion that he might not have complied) or for his possessions? Either way, it is little to his credit that the safety of his family comes so low in his list of priorities. This is by no means the only place in scripture where men use their wives or other women as a human shield. (Compare Genesis 12:10–13; 19:4–8; 20:2, 11; 26:7; Judges 4:17–20; 19:22–24; 2 Samuel 15:16; 16:21–22.)

But it is Ben-Hadad who is the subject of the narrator's chief scorn here. As the armies line up for battle, he is sitting in a tent with his allies, drinking (v. 12). This is a surprising detail to read in an otherwise sparse narrative, but it is quickly followed by an intensification – by midday, he is already drunk: 'They went out at noon, and Ben-Hadad was drinking himself drunk in the tents, he and the thirty-two kings helping him' (v. 16). Now follows a genuinely funny moment in the story. When the scouts report an oncoming army, Ben-Hadad is incapable of issuing a coherent instruction. 'If they have come for peace, take them alive. But if they have come for war… take them alive' (v. 18). Unsurprisingly, he and his army are trounced. Round one to Israel, but Ben-Hadad survives to fight another day.

3 No true man

We take a break from the Aram–Israel rivalry to consider the story of Naboth's vineyard. Through our lens of humour, some additional nuances emerge.

First, notice the description of Ahab in 20:43 as 'ill-humoured and sullen', an unusual pair of words which is used of him again after Naboth's refusal (21:4). The rare word root translated 'sullen' (*sar*) is used of the disobedient son in Deuteronomy 21:18–19, and there are other indicators that Ahab is acting – in contemporary terms – like a sulky teenager. Note how he takes to his bed and turns his face to the wall (v. 4). His wife placates him (v. 7), beginning with two soothing words, 'Now, you' (Hebrew pronunciation *atar atar*). Further baby-talk follows, where Jezebel eschews standard grammar, literally saying, 'It's you that does the kinging in Israel.' Her actions on his behalf, and her redacted account of them (vv. 8–14, compare. vv. 7, 15) are like a mother who is ruthless in advancing her child's cause while taking care to shield him from the murkier details.

Additionally, there are textual hints that represent Ahab as an emasculated man. In this ancient society, Jezebel's authority and autonomy are surprising. 'She wrote letters in Ahab's name and she sealed them with his seal' (v. 8). Only in one other place do we encounter an individual writing a letter on behalf of a king and sealing the letter with his seal (Esther 3:10–12; 8:2, 7–10). There, however, the edicts had been directly commanded by the king. Here, Ahab is ignorant (or demonstrates plausible deniability) of Jezebel's actions.

The elders' absolute obedience to Jezebel's orders is emphasised by the close match between instruction and fulfilment (vv. 12–13; compare vv. 9–10), even to the point of using non-standard grammatical forms. And, even though the letter is sent as from Ahab, the reply comes to Jezebel (v. 14; compare v. 8). Clearly it is an open secret that she acts in his name.

One further piece of evidence that Ahab is emasculated is found in the prophet's condemnation. Literally, it reads, 'I will cut off unto Ahab that which urinates against a wall' (v. 21). The vulgar expression occurs six times in the Hebrew Bible, each time referring to the extermination of an entire male line ('I will cut off from Ahab everyone who urinates standing up'). The literal reading of the phrase would be that it refers to the removal of the male genitalia – which, of course, would also result in the termination of the family line.

Juvenile or emasculated, this king who uses his wife to steal from his neighbour is no true man.

4 Exposing the Lord's will, and the king's

1 Kings 22:1–28

Another year, another confrontation between Ahab and Ben-Hadad, this time provoked by the Israelites (v. 3). Piqued by the loss of some territory that Israel had previously owned, Ahab seeks to talk the king of Judah into an alliance against Aram. But Jehoshaphat, very wisely, won't go to war without consulting God. Enter the court prophets, all 400 of them. And, as one man, they commend the king's plan (v. 6).

Jehoshaphat, however, smells a rat. 'Is there no other prophet of the Lord for us to ask?' (v.7). Ahab's reply is unexpectedly frank. There is Micaiah, he concedes, 'But I hate him, because he never prophesies good for me, only bad' (v. 8). So Micaiah is summoned.

The next scene is pure comic theatre. Centre stage are Ahab and Jehoshaphat, enthroned in all their kingly splendour, with the 400 court prophets working themselves up into a frenzy before them (compare 1 Kings 18:26–29). One, a certain Zedekiah, is charging about with iron horns to represent the way that the kings will gore their enemies (v. 11).

Micaiah is not part of this tableaux. He has to be summoned, demonstrating that he is not in the pay (and hence the pocket) of the king. It is less cushy to be independent, but it means he can speak truth to power. And so it proves, for when the messenger comes with the warning to match his words to the other prophets' (v. 13), he responds as a true prophet ought. 'As the Lord lives, what the Lord says to me, that I will speak' (v. 14; compare Numbers 22:18; 24:13; Ezekiel 2:3–5).

Micaiah's words to the king cause some Bible readers consternation. Doesn't he lie to him? 'Go up and triumph. The Lord will give the battle into the king's hand' (v. 15). But Ahab's response (v. 16) shows that he detects Micaiah's sarcasm. More than this, though, it forces him to expose his own duplicity. He didn't want the Lord's true word (v. 8) but now he is forced to ask for it. And despite the stern warning that heeding the 400 will lead to his downfall (vv. 19–23), he goes to battle anyway. Because, in the end, his mind was already made up. You can find out how that went in verses 34–37.

5 'These are not the men you are looking for'

Ahab has been succeeded by Ahaziah, but the rivalry between Aram and Israel continues. Ben-Hadad is frustrated that Elisha seems to be able to hear his top-secret plans and warn Ahaziah about them. As one of his officers says: 'He tells the king of Israel the words you speak in your bedroom' (v. 12)! So Ben-Hadad sends an attachment of soldiers to seize the prophet, and they surround the city of Dothan where Elisha is holed up with his servant.

Now follows a medley of miracles involving sight and blindness. The servant is dismayed to see the enemy, but at Elisha's prayer the heavenly army is revealed to him (v. 17). Elisha then goes out to the enemy, who have been struck blind at his prayer. The narrative then takes a bizarre turn as Elisha offers to (mis)direct them: 'This is not the way, and this is not the city. Follow me and I will bring you to the man you are seeking' (v. 19). At Elisha's suggestion, the blind soldiers trustingly follow him…

… into the presence of the king of Israel, the very enemy they are ultimately seeking to defeat. This is a dangerous moment for them. Surely Ahaziah will take the opportunity to kill them or, at the very least, disgrace them (compare 1 Chronicles 19:4). But the king of Israel seems perplexed: 'Shall I smite them, smite them, my father?' (v. 21). Of course not! Elisha chides. Throw them a feast! So the king does, and his enemy departs with the obligation of hospitality upon them (v. 23).

Scripture frequently uses the motifs of blindness and deafness as metaphors for spiritual dullness (compare Mark 8:17–29). Here, only the prophet truly 'sees', and everyone else is stumbling in the dark, though as these two chapters show, it is a blindness of their own making.

6 Folly in high places

2 Kings 6:24–25, 7:1–20

His men may have enjoyed Ahaziah's royal hospitality, but to Ben-Hadad this is a humiliation which he won't take lying down. This time it is Israel's capital, Samaria, which he has placed under siege; a siege so brutal that its inhabitants resort to cannibalism (see 2 Kings 6:26–29). But the situation will not last, God reassures the people through Elisha. Soon basic food staples will be in such abundance that they will be devalued, in contrast to the enormously inflated prices of even the most unappetising foods during the siege (7:1; compare 6:25 – 'dove's dung' probably refers to milled chickpeas).

Such a promise is ludicrous to the king's chief military strategist. 'Look, even if God made windows in the heavens, could this be?' (7:2). And of course, it would seem ludicrous to him. For just as God instructed Gideon to reduce the size of his army from 32,000 to 300 (Judges 7:1–8), just as God through Zechariah promises a great work 'not by might, nor by power, but by my Spirit' (Zechariah 4:6), so here, too, military victory is entirely out of the hands of this mighty man. His mocking words about windows (*arubbah*) are echoed in the four (*arba'*) lepers who lift the siege. The mighty Arameans flee in terror (7:7, 15) because they think the Egyptians (*mitzrayim*) are upon them, when in fact, it is just four bumbling lepers (*metzora'iym*) who stumble into the abandoned camp. Who's the fool there?

As always, God confounds the wisdom of the 'wise' and subverts the boasts of those who think they are powerful (compare 1 Corinthians 1:18–31).

Guidelines

When reading Old Testament narratives, it is unwise to attempt to draw a 'lesson' from each short pericope. Instead, it is important to read patiently, looking for emerging themes and always seeking to place the small narrative into the context of the large. Our studies this week have uncovered at least two important themes.

First, our narrator has used humour – sometimes quite sharp humour – to uncover the folly, arrogance and lack of integrity of many characters within our text. But note that this critique is not confined to the pagan 'others', such as Ben-Hadad. God's covenant people are always held to the highest standards of all (compare Luke 12:48; James 4:17).

Second, note the divine action to avert war in several of these texts. God uses Micaiah's bold sarcasm to warn against aggressive action (1 Kings 22:15–28); he allows Elisha to operate as a supernatural spy to avert ambushes (2 Kings 6:8–10); he tricks the Arameans and shames the Israelites into feasting rather than fighting (2 Kings 6:14–23); and he dupes the besieging Arameans into panicked flight (2 Kings 7:6–7), shaming the boasts of men of war on both sides. For those who are troubled by divine sanction for violence elsewhere in the Old Testament, this will be welcome indeed.

FURTHER READING

Helen Paynter, *Reduced Laughter: Seriocomic features and their functions in the book of Kings* (Brill, 2016).

Helen Paynter, 'Ahab – Heedless Father, Sullen Son: Humour and intertextuality in 1 Kings 21', *Journal for the Study of the Old Testament 41:4*, 2017, pp. 451–74.

Helen Paynter, *The Strange World of Elijah and Elisha* (Grove Books, 2019).

Work and rest in Matthew's gospel

Stephanie Addenbrooke Bean

'Work' is a strange word. Its definition varies across cultures and its meaning is coded differently for every single person. In most cases, a person's understanding of work is defined by their employment status. If they like their job, they may have a favourable opinion of work. But if their situation is different, work may be more of a burden than a source of joy. If this stressful work brings sufficient (or excess) money, the burden may be perceived as 'worth it'. But if it doesn't, the work can appear futile. Some people work to enable an 'outside of work' lifestyle they long for, whereas others find their purpose in their work.

Rest is often intertwined with all of this. Work and rest are set up almost like polar opposites – rest is what one does when one is not working. So, when we read verses such as, 'Come to me, all you who are weary and burdened, and I will give you rest' (Matthew 11:28), we can easily interpret this to mean that Jesus will meet us when we are not working, and that therefore work is something Christians need to lay down in order to fully rest in Jesus.

The passages I have selected from Matthew present us with a perspective that will hopefully shift our understanding of work and rest. I posit that work is not inherently bad, as Adam and Eve worked in the garden (Genesis 2). It is our attitude and our attachment to work that need evaluation. When approached wisely, rest in Jesus is possible even as we work. In fact, it is necessary. Rest is found when we seek the priceless treasures in heaven as opposed to racing after the pennies of this world.

Unless otherwise stated, Bible quotations are taken from the NIV.

1 No hesitation

Matthew 4:18–22

It perhaps seems odd to begin a study of work by looking at people who left it. When Jesus calls Simon Peter, Andrew, James and John, they 'immediately' leave their boats to follow a new calling. It makes me wonder: were they so bad at fishing that leaving their nets was a relief? Did they find their job so boring that following a relatively unknown itinerant preacher seemed exciting? Maybe James and John were just fed up of working with their dad! Or was something else going on that caused them to be compelled to follow Jesus? Whatever the reason, the first disciples were open to Jesus' call.

Being a fisherman was a common job. It probably brought in enough money for a stable lifestyle, even if it wasn't particularly flashy. The fact that the first disciples left their boats without hesitation means they had more than a passive interest in following Jesus. They were willing to sacrifice stability and security. For some of us (myself included), knowing what will happen tomorrow has become the greatest source of security. For others, money is the primary motivator. And many of us struggle with Jesus' admonition that 'anyone who loves their father or mother more than me is not worthy of me' (10:37). Jesus demands sacrifice, and that can be difficult to sit with.

But Jesus doesn't expect the disciples to have it all figured out when they follow him. He says, knowing that they are fishermen, 'I will send you out to fish for people' (v. 19). The call isn't a complicated, multiple-page job description. It's a simple invitation using images they'll understand. And there's an implication of training and preparation – 'Come, follow me… and I will send you out' (v. 19). There is no expectation that the first disciples would know instantly how to take on this calling. The Greek word *kai* (translated here simply as 'and') could also be translated as 'and then', suggesting Jesus is not demanding an immediate turnaround. Jesus will take care of them in their calling.

Not every follower of Jesus is called to 'fish for people' in the way that these disciples were, but all can learn from them regardless. They came 'at once' (v. 20) when Jesus called. There was no hesitation, and that response is worth emulating.

2 The secret life

Matthew 6:1–24

While we may not wish to admit it, so many of our conversations about work are performative. We live in a hustle culture that rewards those who log the most hours, assuming that hours spent in the office directly correlates to one's commitment to the role. Working hard is good and sometimes our jobs require extra hours, but these passages in Matthew implore us to consider how we tell the story. Here, Jesus is condemning those who claim to do good when their hearts are not in the right place. Are we loudly and proudly proclaiming that we've barely slept or haven't taken a day off for the sake of working harder? If so, what message are we sending to those around us? In some ways, this kind of talk is akin to the prayers of the hypocrites, for it begs the question: what reward are we seeking when we boast in our own perceived self-righteousness?

Towards the end of today's selected passages, Jesus says, 'Do not store up for yourselves treasures on earth… but store up for yourselves treasures in heaven… for where your treasure is, there your heart will be also' (vv. 19–21). Sometimes our chosen treasures are financial, and this is a common interpretation of these verses. But many (if not all) of us have craved the approval of others instead of relying on heavenly grace. God does not require us to hustle to receive his love and praise, yet many of us act as if this is the case.

The Lord's Prayer teaches us to value simplicity and humility. Its context in the sermon on the mount is often forgotten. Jesus teaches prayer as an antidote to hypocrisy. It is an individual practice, acknowledging that 'your Father knows what you need before you ask him' (v. 8). Prayer, therefore, is not solely a practice of petition but a discipline of worship.

3 The active pursuit

The final verses of this passage are the classic verses cited when Christians talk about rest: 'Come to me, all you who are weary and burdened, and I will give you rest' (v. 28). In the context of this study on work, it could be easy to set these verses up as an aspiration for our non-working lives. I could say that when our working hours come to an end, it is then that we go to Jesus and take to him the burdens from the day. Or that it is only when our burdens have become so overwhelming that we need Jesus' rest. But this passage, particularly when read in context, ought to teach us to be perpetually seeking Jesus' rest and that seeking rest is very much an active process.

There are four verbs of instruction across verses 28 and 29: come, take, learn, find. Three of those require the initiative of the hearer. It is us who must come, take and learn. Then we will find the rest Jesus provides. But it is not simply given. In verse 20, Jesus 'began to denounce the towns in which most of his miracles had been performed, because they did not repent'. In these towns, the crowds came to Jesus, bringing the sick and seeing them be healed. Many of them were surely weary and burdened. But they did not receive the rest in return. They opted out by deciding not to repent. Repentance is a choice, but so is avoiding it. By denouncing those who did not repent, Jesus warns his followers against passive engagement in his ministry.

Finding rest in Jesus can take work, which feels counterintuitive. But this is where our definition of work is important. If we conceive of work as something that requires effort then, yes, finding rest in Jesus takes work. This line of thinking can easily slip into legalism (which I intend to avoid), but it is worth acknowledging that the true rest found in Jesus comes out of an active pursuit. We need to learn from Jesus, which means knowing him. His yoke is easy and his burden is light (v. 30), but we will never find it if we only occasionally search. Jesus tells us himself that when we come to him, he will be ready to relieve us of our burdens. It seems wise to do this every day.

4 Giving it all up

The instruction from Jesus to the wealthy man in Matthew 19 to sell his possessions and give to the poor is striking and certainly challenging. In verse 21, Jesus asks the man if he wants to be perfect. That seems quite a tall order! This is not necessarily moral perfection. The Greek word here (τέλειος) tends to refer to a sense of end or completion. So it could be argued that Jesus is referring to reaching one's *telos* as a Christian. Whether that in itself is perfection can be debated. My point, though, is that Jesus is encouraging the man to consider his ultimate aspirations. It seems the wealthy man wants to unlock eternal life as one might unlock the next level in a video game. Jesus wants the man to consider a change that will require daily sacrifice. Selling one's possessions and giving to the poor may appear to be a one-time event, but it is perhaps better for us to understand it as a lifelong commitment. It requires a complete character shift and a reorientation of values. The disciples are also instructed to reorientate their values when, at the end of this passage, Jesus tells them, 'Many who are first will be last, and many who are last will be first' (v. 30).

This passage is far more complex than a comment on having wealth. It's about values. This young man chooses to leave Jesus, despondent, as opposed to following him (in stark contrast to the invitation to the first disciples, who came 'at once', 4:20). He determines that a lifestyle change (temporary while on earth) is not worth the chance at eternal life. This is perhaps why it is easier for a camel to fit through the eye of a needle than a rich person to enter the kingdom of God (v. 24). The rich person isn't willing to let go of the money.

There are other passages in scripture which instruct us on how to handle money. It seems, though, that this passage in Matthew might be about values. So, when thinking about work, the question remains: are you willing to rest, to come to Jesus and to follow him? Work (whatever that looks like) has come to define so many of us. Would you walk away sad if Jesus told you to give it up?

5 Bearing fruit

The instance of Jesus overturning tables is one of the few events recorded in all four gospels, usually signalling the beginning of Jesus' path to his crucifixion. Jesus is now in Jerusalem, having arrived triumphantly to cries of 'Hosanna in the highest heaven!' (21:9) Yet it seems to all go downhill from here. We should not simply interpret this event as an example of appropriate anger. There is much to learn here about the temple and the changes that Jesus' death and resurrection bring to our worship – there is no longer a need for moneychangers or doves in a post-resurrection world. Regarding a theology of work, this is massively significant. Does this mean that we should refuse to engage in faith-based work that brings in money? Jesus calls the moneychangers thieves for selling within the temple courts. What's the difference? One might argue there isn't one.

The next day (according to Matthew), Jesus curses a fig tree. This isn't unrelated to the overturning of the tables. The fig tree wasn't producing fruit – '[Jesus] went up to it but found nothing on it except leaves' (v. 19). In scripture, fruit is a common image to describe someone's faith life. For example, the fruit of the Spirit are the traits one should hope to find in someone who is fruitful (Galatians 5:22–23). So the fact that this tree has no fruit and only leaves can be interpreted as a reminder that a faith without fruit is not really a faith at all. So when Jesus overturns the tables in the temple, he is proclaiming that the moneychangers' work is not producing fruit. They are operating in the 'house of prayer' (v. 13), but their work is not glorifying God.

So, considering the question of whether we can endorse money-making Christian endeavours, the answer is the same as with secular work: is it producing fruit? This is not just a question to ask of organisations. It is worth asking ourselves as individuals too. And we cannot bear fruit if we do not rest. This is what Jesus tells us in 11:28–30. That's why those passages are actually so difficult. It can be hard to imagine rest when bearing fruit can feel like an active process that requires work. The good news is that the fruit of the Spirit overflows from resting in Jesus – so it's good to rest.

6 Go tell the world

Matthew 28:16–20

The great commission, the closing verses in the gospel of Matthew, is Jesus' final instruction to his disciples, one that we are invited to follow also. And it is an instruction that requires an active response: 'Go and make disciples of all nations, baptising them in the name of the Father and of the Son and of the Holy Spirit, and teaching them to obey everything I have commanded you' (vv. 19–20). It can be easy to get caught up in the verbs of the great commission, using it as an excuse to put all our effort into doing things for Jesus. But note the first word of verse 19. It says 'therefore', which means we need to look at the phrase before. The great commission overflows from the fact that 'all authority in heaven and on earth' belongs to Jesus (v. 18). We are instructed to go and make disciples because of this. The great commission is bookended with reminders that Jesus has authority and that he is with us – 'Surely I am with you always, to the very end of the age' (v. 20). So it is actually not about us at all. It is about who Jesus is.

The great commission, it seems, is intended to be our response to Jesus. We should want to pursue the actions listed in these verses because they are a natural extension of knowing the truth about Jesus. To use the image from the last study, this is our fruit. It does often require effort and intentionality, and for some of us it is part of our employment and our vocation. But, regardless of what we do during the day, making disciples should come as an outpouring of our individual relationship with Jesus. And that relationship needs to be grounded in the rest that only Jesus can provide, so that when we come to him 'weary and burdened' (11:28), we are being renewed and replenished by the one who has 'all authority in heaven and on earth' (v. 18) and who has promised to be with us 'to the very end of the age' (v. 20).

Guidelines

It seems that rest is more complicated than we might like to think, and goes beyond putting one's feet up. It is about an active engagement with Jesus. And this can take effort, which, I will not deny, is work. It is important, then, to distinguish between employment and activity. But more important than categorising our schedules, Matthew's gospel encourages us to evaluate the role that these things have in our lives – both publicly and privately.

- The hypocrites (Matthew 6) and the wealthy man (Matthew 19) had all 'the right things' but were unwilling to make the lifestyle changes and personal sacrifices required to devote their lives fully to following Jesus. The fig tree that Jesus curses only had leaves. Are you bearing fruit? What aspects of your lifestyle might God be challenging you to re-evaluate in this next season so that you are more fruitful?

- In Matthew 4 and 28, Jesus tasks the disciples with following him. This is not a passive activity. Following Jesus is sometimes a laborious journey. We see this in the lives of the twelve disciples when Jesus sends them out in Matthew 10. However, Matthew 11 reminds us that we cannot simply follow Jesus' instructions; we must also rest in him. Rest is perhaps not the best word to use, as it can evoke the image of not doing anything. While rest sometimes demands stillness, it is not the only way to rest. So we must 'abide' in him (John 15:4–11, NRSV; NIV uses 'remain'). And we must choose to do so. How might you integrate rest into your daily rhythm? What does it look like for you to rest in Jesus?

- Importantly, the study of work and rest in Matthew's gospel reveals that such categories of work and rest are not diametrically opposed, nor are they the worldly categories of 'working/not working'. They are complex words and terms that demand individual interrogation. What does work mean to you? What is your definition, and is it a good one?

FURTHER READING

Claudia Hammond, *The Art of Rest: How to find respite in the modern age* (Canongate Books, 2019).

Esther Reed, *Good Work: Christian ethics in the workplace* (Baylor University Press, 2010).

Nicola Slee, *Sabbath: The hidden heartbeat of our lives* (Darton, Longman and Todd, 2019).

1 Samuel 16—31:
Saul and David, paranoia and providence

Walter Moberly

Previously in 1 Samuel: Saul has become the first king of Israel, after being chosen and anointed by the prophet Samuel. However, despite starting well, Saul has failed to wholeheartedly adhere to the Lord. Consequently, he has been told by Samuel that the Lord has 'rejected' him from being king. Nonetheless, Saul remains in position as king, though one imagines him to be wary about what the future will bring.

The overall theme in 1 Samuel 16—31 is the relationship (or rather non-relationship) between Saul and his prospective successor, designated secretly by Samuel and feared openly by Saul: David. Although David will become Israel's greatest king, and in a certain sense is the model for a future messiah, his story is challenging. David's deep trust in the Lord is made clear at the outset. Yet when he is on the run from a hostile Saul, his survival strategy raises many moral and spiritual questions. Evaluating David is made harder by the silence of the narrator, who tells the story without passing evaluative comment, even when we would find it most helpful. There may be tension between moral values we would naturally bring to bear, values formed by our Christian faith, and a desire to hear the story on its own terms.

Those of us who live in secure life situations should be slow to find fault with the actions of those for whom survival is, literally, a life-and-death struggle against murderous opposition; we may not understand what we are talking about. We need to remember that God, not any of us, is Judge, now and on the last day. We also need to learn more about the nature of life, and about good and evil, from a difficult portion of scripture and to read wisely and morally but not moralisingly.

Bible quotations are taken from the NRSV.

1 Surface appearances deceive

1 Samuel 16:1–13

Samuel's grief over Saul's failure gives way to a fresh start. But Samuel is dismayed by the Lord's commission. People with power often try to protect it by becoming deadly towards rivals and those who support them. The Lord does not tell Samuel to lie but instead instructs him to be economical with the truth: inviting people in Bethlehem to a sacrifice should sound harmless and not provoke Saul should he hear of it (vv. 1–5).

Initially, everyone makes a mistaken judgement (vv. 6–10). Jesse does not bother to include David, his youngest son, when summoned by Samuel to come with his sons to the sacrifice; he clearly assumes that youngest means insignificant. Yet Samuel too gets it wrong, when impressed by Eliab's good looks and impressive stature (like Saul, back in the day, 10:23). The Lord reminds him that the truth about human reality, the heart and mind that make us the people we are, is not a matter of outward appearance. Rather, it is something only God clearly knows; though of course we can learn something of people's inner reality through their words and especially their actions. In today's world, we have exacerbated the problem, as so much of contemporary life – advertising, entertainment, sexually active lifestyles – is premised on the power and lure of the outwardly attractive. But it is character and disposition that count.

Once that principle is confirmed to Samuel, the chosen son is in fact attractive in appearance (v. 12). If good looks are no reliable guide to good character, they are also not incompatible with it.

Although anointing becomes a formal mark of a king – as Saul had previously been anointed king by Samuel (10:1), thereby making a king 'an anointed one' (Hebrew *māshiah*, or 'messiah') – it was also the mark of a priest and could presumably be applied to others also (precedents were few in that context). Interestingly, Samuel apparently says nothing by way of explaining his anointing of Jesse's youngest son. So presumably Jesse, his sons and everyone else remained puzzled. David had been singled out and marked – but for what? He returns to his sheep. Only over time, as the Lord's Spirit enables David, will the real meaning of that day become apparent.

2 A tragic story can start so well

1 Samuel 16:14–23; 17:55–58

We read of the first meeting between Saul and David in 16:14–23. Saul is clearly unaware of what happened at Bethlehem and comes to know David simply as someone who is helpful to him through skilful music-making when he feels troubled. It is the one and only time when Saul is well disposed towards David.

This account of David's introduction to Saul stands in some tension with the next chapter, where David appears to be an untried shepherd boy, especially in the final scene, where he appears unknown to Saul (17:55–58). It is not clear how best to handle this. Of course, the description of David as a 'warrior' (16:18), which at this stage in the story is hardly appropriate to a young shepherd, might just be Saul's servant 'talking up' David in terms designed to appeal to Saul. Beyond this, some think there were simply differing accounts of David's introduction that were preserved together despite some inconsistency. Others look for a possibly surprising logic within the storyline. Maybe Saul's already-disintegrating character makes him fail to recognise a David he already knows. Or maybe, when he sees David going out to fight Goliath, Saul remembers that he had heard something about a ceremony conducted by Samuel with Jesse and his sons and suddenly, for the first time, Saul sees a possible horrible significance in it, if perhaps Samuel had anointed one of those sons as he had once anointed Saul: '*Whose* son is this?!'

There is also the question of how to understand the spirit from the Lord that afflicts Saul (16:14, 23). Sadly, the NRSV, like many other translations, is misleading in translating the Hebrew adjective *ra*, that describes the spirit, as 'evil'. The Hebrew terms for 'good' and 'bad' (*tōv* and *ra*) are as wide-ranging and varied in meaning as the English terms. Often *ra* essentially means 'unwelcome'. 'Morally bad', i.e. 'evil', is certainly a possible sense, but only if the context indicates its appropriateness. In this context, Saul has already lost the Lord's favour and is now troubled, and God's engaging with him only furthers this. In our terms, he has an uneasy conscience and can no longer find rest in God. In translational terms, we should think of 'a troubling spirit' from the Lord, to depict a man whose relationship with God is now troubled.

3 Where is real strength to be found?

1 Samuel 17:1–51

(This passage is longer than normal, but it is worth reading the whole thing. If time is an issue, start at verse 19.)

The scene is set with a standoff between the Israelites and the Philistines. The Philistine champion, Goliath, is a kind of tank on legs. He is characterised by defiance, a scorn for Israel, that is a repeated motif of the story (vv. 10, 25, 26, 45). He also proposes to resolve the standoff via single combat – winner takes all. This could be a great moment for Saul as Israel's king. But he and his men are characterised by the motif of fear (vv. 11, 24, 32).

Enter David, who is running errands for his father. His enquiries about what is going on meet with dismissive rejection from his brother, one of Saul's fearful soldiers. Yet David sees things differently from others: it is Goliath's defiance, not his massive strength, that concerns him. He is not afraid.

When he is brought before Saul, we have David's first keynote speech (vv. 34–37). In Hebrew narrative, the speeches of the main figures at critical moments regularly reveal inner character and give the key to understanding the story. How can David persuade Saul to let him represent Israel? He tells of his overcoming animals that are usually deadly to humans, and how he sees Goliath as hardly different. Crucially, he ascribes his success not to himself but to the Lord who is with him. Saul commissions him as Israel's champion.

There is then the comical attempt to get David to face Goliath with routine military strength: armour and sword. Maybe David goes along with this to humour Saul, though maybe he genuinely doesn't yet know how he should face Goliath. Either way, David soon makes a key resolution: he must use the ordinary things he already knows.

As David goes out to confront Goliath, perhaps taking his staff to confuse Goliath as though it were his weapon, he makes his second keynote speech (vv. 45–47): Goliath reckons on the power of conventional weapons, but David knows a deeper truth, and what happens that day will enable others to know it too.

David's trust in God's surprising power does not excuse him from still playing his part. An insignificant-looking sling can, in the hands of someone who knows how to use it, be a deadly weapon. David probably stuns Goliath with his stone and then, with supreme irony, uses Goliath's own sword to finish him off.

Strength in apparent weakness becomes a scriptural keynote.

4 Saul resents David

1 Samuel 18:1—19:7

Saul keeps David at court and gives him military command, perhaps initially on the principle of making the most of David's exceptional abilities. But the narrator quickly tells us of Saul's jealousy (18:8–9), and it is possible that this is an element in Saul's retaining David from the outset, especially if he is nervous about what Samuel did with this son of Jesse the Bethlehemite (18:2; 17:58). Is Saul operating on the principle of 'keep your friends close, and your enemies closer'? It looks as though very soon, if not already from the outset, Saul gives David military command in the hope that the Philistines will do to David what Saul himself would really like to do (18:17, an idea tragically also used by David himself later on against Uriah; see 2 Samuel 11). Indeed, on a bad day of feeling troubled, Saul, no longer grateful for David's soothing music, does try to kill David (18:10–11); though here, as subsequently, David always manages to keep a step ahead of Saul.

Quite the opposite of Saul is his son Jonathan, for whom David is as special as could be (18:1, 3–4). Their friendship will play a key role in the next few chapters, as together Jonathan and David seek to work out whether there is any future for David at Saul's court (an initial episode of which is 19:1–7). The people of Israel also esteem and favour David (18:16), as does Saul's daughter Michal, who is happy to become his wife (18:20, 28).

Someone exceptional who does great things for people, and is loved by them, yet who is also resented and feared – this is not an uncommon pattern in life (one might think perhaps of Abraham Lincoln or Mahatma Gandhi). It is supremely present in the portrayal of Jesus in the gospels. In his teaching, healing and table fellowship, Jesus is consistently giving himself to others. Yet although some love him and find life and joy, others see him as a threat. The fear is irrational, yet that makes it no less potent. Jesus' giving life to Lazarus (John 11:1–44) leads directly into a strategic decision that Jesus must be got rid of (John 11:45–53).

David is thereby, in a certain sense, a figural anticipation of Jesus. There remains a lasting challenge as to whether we can truly recognise and appreciate what, or who, is life-giving when it is before our eyes.

5 David starts to live on the run

We pass over two chapters (19:8—20:42) in which the issue of whether David can remain at Saul's court in reasonable safety is worked out. The answer is a clear no. For the foreseeable future, David must be a fugitive and live by his wits.

Saul's enmity towards David is apparently not yet widely known, and this enables David to be plausibly deceptive when he comes to Ahimelech at a temple at Nob: he is on a secret mission and needs some food for himself and his men. (The narrative generally gives the impression that David is on his own. But there is a passing reference to accompanying young men [21:4–5], and when Jesus refers to this story, he reads it as telling of both David and companions [Mark 2:23–27]). The only available food is holy bread, which according to Israel's law is reserved for priests (Leviticus 24:5–9). But Ahimelech is willing to meet the presenting need, as long as David and his men have at least a certain level of ritual purity, which David claims they indeed have. Ahimelech's willingness to set aside certain ritual requirements when there is human need is endorsed by Jesus as showing a wise set of priorities.

David also wants a weapon, and the only weapon at this shrine, Goliath's sword, has ironically become a sacred object, carefully wrapped and preserved. (How the sword got there we do not know, but the Philistines also deposit in a temple the armour of a defeated enemy, 31:9–10). David takes Goliath's sword, though the narrative subsequently never draws attention to it.

David's deception of Ahimelech appears successful. Moving on, he also deceives the Philistine Achish by the bizarre expedient of plausibly acting so crazily that he could not be considered a threat. Moving on again, he gathers more followers, as he looks to be a good option for people who have fallen into hard times. He also takes the sensible precaution of protecting his parents from Saul's possible malice by sending them to the land of his great-grandmother, Ruth (22:3–4).

David's living by his wits with 'needs must' behaviour looks to be going well. But… and there is a big 'but', as we will see tomorrow. This is the mentioned-in-passing presence of Doeg (21:7). David's success may not be what it seems.

6 Mass murder

Earlier in 1 Samuel, when Saul loses the Lord's favour, many a reader will feel some sympathy for him, because his failure does not seem great. Here, however, we encounter a Saul who forfeits any sympathy. He becomes a mass murderer.

The key figure is Doeg, previously just mentioned in passing as present at Nob when David was speaking with Ahimelech (21:7). Here we encounter him as one of Saul's loyalists. When Saul, in his paranoia and self-pity, is looking around for someone on whom to focus his displeasure (22:8–9), Doeg offers up the name of Ahimelech as someone whom he knows to have offered practical assistance to David. So Saul instantly summons to Gibeah not only Ahimelech but every other priest at Nob who might possibly have assisted him (and it was clearly a substantial community, with 85 priests), and interrogates them.

Ahimelech makes a straightforward defence: he was not to know that Saul considered David a rebel, and he had acted in ignorance. In his irrational paranoia, Saul simply dismisses this: if Ahimelech has helped David, then that makes him a traitor. Saul then orders a mass execution, on the grounds that all the other priests must also have been involved (paranoia needs no evidence). Saul's servants, however, refuse; they presumably have an intuitive sense that to kill priests on the flimsy grounds of the king's paranoia would be a terrible offence against God and would be worse for them than facing Saul's anger. Doeg, however, has no such compunction. Either single-handedly, or more likely with a few loyalists of his own (though the narrator focuses on Doeg as the key figure), he not only murders the priests, but also goes to their hometown of Nob and slaughters everyone there. Only one priest, Abiathar, escapes and finds David and tells him what happened.

But now comes a remarkable twist. David says he knew not only that Doeg was at Nob but also that he was likely to tell Saul. Perhaps it's essentially a strong way of saying, 'It's all my fault.' Taken at face value, however, it could mean that David's lying to Ahimelech was to give Ahimelech the defence of 'plausible deniability', if questioned. Moreover, Ahimelech himself might have known of David's real situation: why else should he have trembled (21:1)?

The narrative suggests that things are not always as they may appear at first sight. But it also shows that David's wiliness can have terrible unintended consequences.

Guidelines

Although they have been much read and commented on down the ages, the David narratives are still not easy to read well. The biblical writers make demands on their readers, and their conventions can, at this distance, sometimes seem opaque.

We have seen it is not quite clear what is really going on when David speaks to Ahimelech, because the narrative is intrinsically open to more than one reading. And it is easy to misinterpret, and so mistranslate, the 'bad' spirit.

Sometimes, however, well-meaning readers can stumble. I have come across the proposal that it was a wobble in David's faith when he chose five stones (17:40); if he really trusted God, one should have sufficed. This is surely wrong in a story where everything else that David says and does, especially in his two keynote speeches, affirms his strong trust in God. When David takes off Saul's armour in favour of doing what he knows how to do, the picture is of his taking a handful of good stones as a natural preparation for using his sling; it is just normal practice. An incidental detail should not be set against the overall consistent picture.

It is also possible that already in antiquity (it's not just a modern problem!) someone misread David's killing of Goliath: if the Lord does not save by the sword, how come David kills Goliath with a sword? This may explain the unusual comment by the narrator in 17:50 – unusual, because the story is usually allowed to speak for itself, and David's point about the Lord's deliverance could not have been made more clearly (17:47). If one reads 17:49 and 17:51 in sequence without 17:50, there is a smooth account of David's actions, in which the stone probably stuns Goliath before David finishes him off. But if this allows the wooden objection that David actually wins with a sword, the narrator has added a clarifying comment in 17:50, to emphasise that the key element in David's victory, which brought about Goliath's death, was that *there was no sword in David's hand*. Why state the obvious, unless someone is denying it?

David does much that is open to question. But his faithful understanding of God's ways in his most famous story should not be questioned, and should still inform and challenge us today, not least with its paradoxes.

1 Surprising providence

1 Samuel 25

We pass over several chapters which tell of David and his men on the run from Saul in various places across the hilly Judean wilderness near the Dead Sea.

This story of David, Nabal and Abigail is, like others, open to misreading. A modern reader may be tempted to interpret David's request for payment for not harming Nabal's men (vv. 2–8) as a kind of protection racket. Yet this introduces a suspicion that makes it impossible to hear the story as it stands. Rather, we should envisage the difficulties of life in unpoliced territory where casual raiders readily roam and pillage. David and his men had provided some stability and safety in a respectful relationship with Nabal's shepherds (vv. 15–16), such that would make some sharing in a time of celebration appropriate. Mutuality matters; but Nabal selfishly and boorishly refuses to recognise the help he has received. However, even if David's anger is justified, one might still ask whether the form he envisages for it (if taken at face value) is excessive (vv. 22, 34).

Abigail resourcefully goes out to meet David. Her speech to him recognises David as favoured by the Lord, in words whose significance she herself may not have fully appreciated (vv. 28–30; there is some analogy with Simeon's words about Jesus and Mary in the temple, Luke 2:25–35). Her words also introduce a motif that will be important as the story continues: that David should be kept from bloodguilt and inappropriately avenging himself, which seems specifically, albeit implicitly, to envisage not shedding the blood of anyone who belongs to the people of Israel – whether Nabal, Saul or ordinary Israelites (as will become clear subsequently; vv. 26, 31, 33). Because David recognises the wisdom of Abigail's words, he wisely renounces his strong self-imprecation (vv. 22, 34–35).

Abigail also chooses her time carefully in speaking to her husband, i.e. not when he is drunk and might easily lash out. Only in the morning, when Nabal has sobered up, does she speak. Nabal fails to gratefully recognise what Abigail has done but experiences some kind of cold horror within. Nabal's subsequent death is seen to be divine judgement, whereby David recognises divine providence, via Abigail, overruling his own initial intentions (vv. 38–39). God moves in unexpected ways.

2 David spares Saul

1 Samuel 26:1—27:1

In the wilderness, David remains at risk from Saul, who is determined to hunt him down. Even if David has some 400 men, Saul has the resources to muster some 3,000 for his pursuit. Can David hope to consistently elude Saul?

David finds Saul and his soldiers asleep one night, with apparently even the sentries asleep too (or were there no sentries because Saul was so confident in the strength of his superior numbers?), and this offers David what appears to be a golden opportunity. We are not told why David decides to go down into Saul's camp, and perhaps he is in two minds about what to do. Abishai voices the golden opportunity: he would like nothing better than to perform this straightforward service for his leader (26:8). David's response (perhaps influenced by what happened with Abigail and Nabal) is important for our understanding of him (26:9–11). In this life-and-death decision, David resolves not to seek his own obvious benefit. Rather, he will leave his enemy to God, with all that might entail for himself. Specifically, he respects that Saul, anointed by Samuel, is 'the Lord's anointed' (Hebrew *māshiah*, or 'messiah'). (There is an irony for the Christian reader that this phrase is four times used here of Saul, more than it is ever used of David himself!) David shows an understanding of God and his ways that makes him resist 'common sense'.

Then, from a suitably safe distance, David confronts Saul and his commander. He confronts them with the clear evidence that he had them at his mercy and chose to be merciful. David also claims his innocence towards Saul more generally, perhaps reckoning that in this context his words will be heard.

Saul apparently responds favourably. He addresses David as 'my son', and unequivocally acknowledges that he is in the wrong, that he is indebted to David's mercy and that he has acted foolishly (26:21). It is as comprehensive a confession as could be. Finally, he implicitly acknowledges the Lord's hand guiding and enabling David (26:25).

Strikingly, David does not believe a word of it. Or perhaps he recognises that in this mood Saul may mean what he says, but he has become so unstable that his word can no longer be trusted. So he resolves to leave Israelite territory (27:1).

There are times in life when wisdom requires recognising that seemingly heartfelt words may not be reliable.

3 David deceives Achish

1 Samuel 27:1—28:2

David flees to Philistine territory and settles with the same King Achish whom he deceived previously with his pretend madness (21:10–15). Such a ploy could no longer work when David has his 600 men with him, so instead he offers himself as a loyal servant to Achish, willing to conduct raids on Israelite territory, thus serving Achish's purposes and also ensuring that it would appear unthinkable for him ever to return to Israelite territory.

David is consistently deceitful. Although he tells Achish that he has raided the territory of Israel/Judah, he has in fact raided non-Israelite tribes, including Israel's enemy Amalek. David's deception is also undergirded by ruthlessness. To make sure that Achish does not discover the truth of what he is doing, David leaves no survivors of his raids: dead people tell no tales.

This deception is so successful that Achish trusts David to be part of the Philistine army in an upcoming confrontation with Israel. This will pose a major problem for David. Thus far he has consistently managed not to shed any Israelite blood. But if he fights in the Philistine army, such bloodshed will become inevitable. Although David appears to embrace this option (28:2), his words are almost certainly a bluff to conceal the corner he has painted himself into.

Thus the outline of the story. But how should we evaluate what we read? This is a passage where the silence of the narrator is particularly surprising. One consequence, however, is that the text is wide open to be read in markedly different ways. One can read it as showing partisan approval: 'See how cleverly David put one over on that dumb Philistine.' One can read it in the light of Israel's moral code as shamefully self-serving: 'See how David, with neither pity nor mercy, abuses the gifts and responsibilities he has been given.' One can read it as a failure to display that trust in God's overruling that Abigail and David himself have previously articulated (25:29; 26:10): 'See how David's trust in God's care wavers.' For a Christian reader, the force of the second and third readings is surely inescapable.

However much David is in certain ways a model for the people of God and anticipates Jesus as Messiah, we must recognise that at times he is far from exemplary. Israel's scriptures have striking honesty in their portrayal of Israel's greatest king.

4 Saul and the medium/'witch' of Endor

1 Samuel 28:3-25

The narrative focus shifts from David to Saul for what is, in effect, the climactic episode in the portrayal of Saul (the story is told at length with much detail, unlike Saul's death at Gilboa, which is told briefly).

A Philistine army is coming against Israel, and the once bold and confident Saul (1 Samuel 11) is now fearful (as also when the Philistines had Goliath as their champion). Saul wants some guidance from God as to what he should do, but God is silent (v. 6). One might hope that this silence would drive Saul to ask the reasons for it, and maybe find ways to open his heart again. Sadly, Saul instead seeks out a medium so that he can get some guidance from the deceased Samuel. Israel's law is clear that such attempts to get some leverage on insights from beyond this world are unworthy of, and unacceptable in, a people to whom the Lord has made himself known (Deuteronomy 18:9-14).

Two things stand out in the account of what the medium does. First, it works. The woman is somehow able to raise Samuel. The Old Testament in various places recognises that strange things can happen: Egyptian sorcerers can, like Aaron, turn their staffs into snakes (even though his swallows up theirs, Exodus 7:8-13), and when the king of Moab sacrifices his son, power is released (2 Kings 3:26-27). The Old Testament does not try to explain, or explain away, these phenomena. Perhaps disconcertingly, the Old Testament allows the possibility of things one might think should not be possible.

Second, it is useless. The wraith of Samuel does not give Saul the kind of insight or guidance which he hoped for. After pointedly telling Saul of the futility of consulting him if the Lord himself has been silent (vv. 15-16), Samuel reiterates what he said to Saul during his lifetime (v. 17). His final word is the hopelessness of Saul's situation (v. 19). Saul has gained nothing.

The story concludes with details of how the medium cared for Saul by giving him something to eat, despite his initial refusal. It is hard not to read this homely touch as a positive note in this strange story. Even a medium who does what is forbidden may still have good qualities. As so often, the Old Testament resists easy moralising and recognises the complexity of life.

5 David in distress and success

1 Samuel 29:1—30:25

The scene initially reverts to the Philistines, who are preparing for their battle with Israel. The Philistine commanders are, unsurprisingly and indeed rightly, reluctant to have David in their ranks, lest he swap sides mid-battle. Achish, who has been deceived into trusting David, is overruled. David, realising that he is out of the corner he had been painted into, can safely protest his disappointment and then depart with Achish's protestations of trust and goodwill ringing in his ears. David's deception remains entirely successful, and he is also providentially rescued from being in a position where he would have to shed Israelite blood (29:1–11). God is gracious in surprising ways.

On his return to Ziklag, David finds desolation after an Amalekite raid, a desolation so great that his men almost turn against him. David's turning to the Lord to find strength to cope sounds a note that is never sounded of Saul (30:1–6). He also seeks the Lord's guidance to know whether or not he should go after the Amalekites (30:7–8).

In what follows, striking space is given to the account of the Egyptian slave, abandoned and left to die in the desert of the Negeb, who is revived by David's provisions. Of course, he matters because he can give David the information he wants. Nonetheless, there is an implication that care for an ordinary person matters, and that this abandoned slave is the unexpected channel of God's guidance so that David can find those he is looking for (30:11–15). No care, no finding.

The main narrative interest, however, lies in the treatment of the 200 left behind when it comes to the division of the spoil. Instinctive self-interest has a ready decision: only those who fought the battle get the spoil; those who wimped out lose out (30:22). David, however, overrules this self-interest – although it will cost him as well as his men. David shows a lively sense of gratitude to the Lord for guiding, protecting and providing, in a way that challenges and reframes the voice of self-interest (30:23). Those who stayed behind are not to be penalised (which has resonance with Milton's 'They also serve who only stand and wait'). Rather, all who serve shall share equally in the benefits that may come. This sense of what constitutes a community under God is recognised as a principle of enduring value. David here parallels Solomon for wisdom.

6 The deaths of Saul and Jonathan

During his time as king, Saul has all too often shown fear and paranoia. Indeed, after Samuel warned Saul of his imminent death at Philistine hands (28:19), one might perhaps have expected Saul to try to get out of the coming battle: perhaps by a generous offer to the Philistines; perhaps by feigning illness; perhaps by simply fleeing to somewhere safe across the Jordan. But Saul faces his end with courage, and there is a certain tragic dignity in the account of his death.

Very quickly the battle goes in favour of the Philistines, and the Israelites start to fall back. Saul has to endure the death of Jonathan, his heir, and two other sons (the only surviving son is Ishbaal, presumably not present at the battle). Then he himself is wounded, and he realises that his end has come. He does not want the shame of the Philistines crowing over him as they put him to death at their will. His loyal armour-bearer flinches at his master's request, but readily joins his master in death. It's not really suicide (though often read as such), as death is coming; rather, Saul opts to die 'at home rather than away'. The Philistines then duly celebrate their victory and deny the decapitated Saul the dignity of burial.

The last word in this part of the narrative goes to the people of Jabesh-Gilead. They remember how Saul had rescued them from Nahash the Ammonite (1 Samuel 11). So they retrieve the bodies of Saul and his sons and, after puzzlingly burning the corpses (perhaps because of decomposition; cremation was not Israelite practice), though not enough to destroy the bones, they bury the remains and mourn.

Despite the problems of his life, and a kingship that was hardly a success, Saul is honoured by some in his death. This is not only from the people of Jabesh-Gilead. More strikingly and fully, it will be from David himself in his noble and gracious lament over Saul and Jonathan (2 Samuel 1:17–27). The biblical narrative implicitly adopts the practice of not speaking badly about the dead.

Saul's real problem was not Philistines nor David but himself, and this was not resolved in his life. The Christian principle is to entrust the departed to God, whose judgement and mercy is exercised through his knowing of a person in a way that we on earth cannot.

Guidelines

It can be salutary to entertain the thought experiment, 'What would you expect scripture, a holy book, to contain?' If we linger with that, we can come to a fresh appreciation of scripture. Natural expectations of a holy book would surely be along the lines of plenty of clear depictions of God, clear dos and don'ts, clear exemplars of good and evil, and clarity about what to hope for in both time and eternity. And of course there is such content. Yet the point of the thought experiment is to remind us of how much else there is.

1 Samuel in particular gives us a narrative of earthly life in all its frequent unclarity. Despite the strong sense that the sovereign Lord works out his purposes via general providence and particular guidance, God's interactions with humanity are often bafflingly ambiguous. Neither Saul nor David are straightforward characters, either 'good' or 'bad'.

Saul is troubled and paranoid. The occasional depiction of this in terms of a 'bad', i.e. troubling, spirit from the Lord reminds us that the Old Testament does not have the range and nuance of psychological categories that we have available today. Nonetheless, its rooting of Saul's troubledness in God indicates that Saul's deepest difficulty was his inability, despite retaining formal allegiance to the Lord, to relate to the Lord with a trust and obedience that could have healed and changed him. Tragically for Saul, the God who called him became for him more enemy than friend.

David relates to God in a way that Saul does not, and this is at the heart of his most famous story, the encounter with Goliath, which has wide resonance in helping us see how faith in God should change our priorities in life and what counts as faithful action. Yet the practicalities of survival make David not only deceive but also take life.

We can still learn from 1 Samuel. But it should help us realise that our holy book confronts us with the need to discern, to reserve judgement and to trust that God's good purposes are at work, even when we can't see it.

FURTHER READING

Walter Brueggemann, *First and Second Samuel (Interpretation: A Bible commentary for teaching and preaching)* (John Knox Press, 1990).

Stephen Chapman, *1 Samuel as Christian Scripture: A theological commentary* (Eerdmans, 2016).

Robert Gordon, *1 & 2 Samuel: A commentary* (Paternoster Press, 1986).

The end of the world

Ian Paul

Where is the world heading? How will it all end? Are we in the 'end times'? These are questions often asked in the modern world, and many claim that we are in unique times when these questions are singularly appropriate.

However, you don't have to look very far into history to see that people have always asked these questions! Harold Camping hit the headlines a few years ago for making specific predictions about the date of Jesus' return – and then having to offer a new date when the previous one passed without incident. In 1844, William Miller predicted that Jesus would return on 22 October; in response, his followers sold up land and homes, and when the date passed, they experienced a crisis known as The Great Disappointment. Many in Europe in the year 999 expected Jesus to return the following year and convened great gatherings in the fields to prepare.

Others argue that the state of the world shows that we are in the 'end times', with the growth of globalisation, computer technologies that are changing society and the climate crisis. Yet we have faced great crises before – diseases, like the Spanish flu, the Black Death and the plague of Justinian, and wars all through history have had a devastating impact – yet history has not come to an end.

When we look at key passages about the end of the world, it turns out the Bible says something more complex and yet more simple than we might have thought. The anticipation of the 'end times' actually has a central place in Christian discipleship – but it does not involve anything to do with predicting dates or looking for 'signs of the times'! Let's explore these passages together and prepare to be pleasantly surprised.

Bible quotations are taken from the NIV.

1 The end of the world?

Matthew 24:29–35

Jesus teaches his disciples as they sit on the Mount of Olives, overlooking Jerusalem from the east. The language of 'distress' or 'tribulation' (v. 29), the signs of cosmic destruction and the angels gathering the nations at the trumpet call (v. 31), all sound very 'end of the world'!

But such a reading is impossible. In response to the disciples' admiration of the splendour of the temple (24:1), Jesus foretells its complete destruction. In amazement, the disciples ask Jesus two questions: 'When will this happen, and what will be the sign of your coming and of the end of the age?' (v. 3). The word they use for 'coming' is *parousia*, which means the royal presence of the king or emperor after a period of absence. Jesus answers this second question from verse 36 – but until then he is answering the first question about the destruction of the temple.

'The Son of Man coming on the clouds' in verse 30 is a phrase taken from Daniel 7:13: 'In my vision at night I looked, and there before me was one like a son of man, coming with the clouds of heaven. He approached the Ancient of Days and was led into his presence.' This is the passage behind Jesus' repeated reference to himself as the 'Son of Man' – and Daniel sees this person coming *to* the throne of God, not coming *from* it. In other words, Matthew 24:30 is not about Jesus' return, but his ascension! This is confirmed by the solemn statement of Jesus in verse 34 that 'this generation will certainly not pass away until all these things have happened'.

This passage is about the end of the world in one sense – the end of the Jewish world, with the nation gathered around the temple. Within one generation, the temple would be destroyed and the people driven from the land. The cosmic language quoted from Isaiah 13:10 and 34:4 signals God's judgement on his people and the overthrowing of powers; the 'tribes of the land' (see NIV footnote) are those who have rejected Jesus; and the 'angels' are the messengers who proclaim the gospel to the end of the earth. There is certainly a new world coming – one in which people from every nation hear and receive the good news of Jesus the Messiah.

2 A rapturous welcome?

Matthew 24:36–44

In the first half of this chapter, Jesus answered the disciples' first question: 'When will the destruction of the temple take place?' Jesus replies that there will be much suffering, the disciples themselves will be put on trial, the temple will be desecrated and there will be many false messiahs. They are to look for the signs of the times, just as they would look at a fig tree to tell the season – the fig tree a symbol of the temple itself, so the withered fig tree of Matthew 21:18–19 points to the corrupt and unfruitful temple facing judgement.

Now the focus changes, from 'these things' to 'that day', Jesus' *parousia* and the end of the age. We know when '*these* things' are going to happen – within a generation – but 'about *that* day or hour no one knows'. The disciples are to look for the signs of the times related to the temple – but not in relation to Jesus' return. The *parousia* of the Son of Man will come like lightning, without any warning (v. 27).

Jesus says it again and again: 'You do not know' (v. 42); the owner of a house does not know when a thief will come (v. 43); the master returns at an unexpected hour (v. 50); the ten virgins do not know when the bridegroom will come (Matthew 25:1–13). The central illustration in this passage is of Noah and the flood. People were carrying on with their everyday lives, ignoring God and focusing on 'eating and drinking, marrying' (v. 38) when the flood came and took them all away in judgement – and it will be the same when Jesus returns. The account in Genesis emphasises that it was the *wicked* who were taken away – Noah and his family were kept and continued to live on earth – and it will be the same at the *parousia*. So when Jesus comes, I want to be left behind, as it will be the wicked who are taken!

The best way to be ready is to put away your calendar, ignore the latest 'end times' prediction and remember that 'no one knows'. The best preparation is to get on with what God has called you to do today, so that, on whatever 'today' he comes, he finds you a 'faithful and wise servant' (Matthew 24:45).

3 The end-times Spirit

Peter's speech at Pentecost in Acts 2 might not be the first place to turn to understand the 'end times', but it is actually of critical importance. Jesus told the disciples to wait for the gift of the Spirit, who would equip them to be his witnesses (Acts 1:4, 8), and on the day of Pentecost the Spirit has come, with sights and sounds that startle the crowd, who wonder what is going on.

Peter begins his explanation by citing the prophet Joel, who was probably writing during the return from exile described in Ezra and Nehemiah. Joel looks forward to the 'day of the Lord' when, after Israel has suffered for her sins and turned back to God, he will restore the people and bring judgement on the nations. As part of this hope, the Spirit of God is no longer confined to a few – priest, kings, prophets – but is poured out on all the people. What is most striking is that, as he quotes Joel 2:28, Peter alters 'afterwards' to 'in the last days' (v. 17), and he is clear that this is the meaning of Pentecost. The Spirit is God's end-times gift to his people, a first instalment and foretaste of the life of the world to come (Ephesians 1:13–14; Romans 8:23). So when people ask, 'Are we in the end times?', the right answer is 'Yes – we have been since the Day of Pentecost!'

The language of Joel that Peter cites includes cosmic imagery similar to that used by Jesus in Matthew 24:29, signalling not a literal end to the physical world but the overturning of earthly powers as the kingdom of God breaks in. In this new era, it will not be just ethnic Jews who know salvation, but 'everyone who calls on the name of the Lord' (v. 21). For Joel, this 'Lord' is Yahweh, the God of Israel, but for Peter here and Paul in Romans 10:13, this God has been made known in the Lord Jesus. The Israel of God will now come from every nation, anticipated in the list of those who have come to Jerusalem in Acts 2:9–11, realised in the Gentile mission from Acts 15 and visualised in Revelation 7:9: 'From every nation, tribe, people and language, standing before the throne and before the Lamb.'

4 Sleeping in death

1 Thessalonians 4:13–18

The Thessalonians heard the gospel from Paul (Acts 17) and responded with enthusiasm (1 Thessalonians 1:6–8), but they are also worried. They expected Jesus to return soon (Acts 1:11), and teaching about eschatology was clearly part of Paul's gospel. Jesus is Lord, seated at the right hand of the Father, and one day this reality, acclaimed by believers (Romans 10:9; 1 Corinthians 12:3) will be seen by all (Philippians 2:11). But despite Jesus' repeated teaching of delay (Matthew 24:48; 25:5, 19), they are concerned that those who have died before Jesus returns will have missed out.

Paul explains that Jesus' death and resurrection are not only the pattern for our spiritual lives – we have 'died' to sin in baptism and been 'raised' to new life coming out of the water (Romans 6:3–4) – but also for our bodily lives. Those who have died are 'sleeping' in death, and just as we get up in the morning when we awake to the new dawn, so the dead in Christ will awake to the dawn of the new age when he returns (the same Greek word is used for both things; see Matthew 9:9; Mark 1:35; 5:42 and so on). This image is the primary way that the New Testament describes death, and it is the reason why Christians have practised burial of the dead through most of history.

Paul does not describe Jesus' return as a '*second* coming', pairing it with the incarnation, but as a 'descent', pairing it with the ascension. There are no 'signs'; his *parousia* comes suddenly with a 'loud command' (v. 16). There is no need to identify the 'trumpet' with that of Matthew 24:31; trumpets were used to call people to worship, announce war and signal victory. We will be caught up 'in the clouds' that signify God's coming presence and 'in the air' (v. 17) as this is the realm of spiritual power (Ephesians 2:2). There is no suggestion here that we then return to heaven with Jesus; when the emperor comes to a city, the elders go out to greet him, and *they* then turn to accompany him into the city to celebrate his *parousia*, his royal presence there after a long absence. This is not a 'secret rapture' but a public vindication; scripture is clear and consistent: we will 'reign on [a renewed] earth' with him forever (Revelation 5:10)!

5 The millennium: I am all for it!

Revelation 20:1–6

The thousand-year reign of the saints with Jesus in Revelation 20 is one of the most confusing and debated issues in discussion about the 'end times'. There are postmillennialists, amillennialists, dispensational mid-tribulation rapture premillennialists – the list goes on! Personally, I am a pro-millennialist – I am all for it. Or perhaps I am a pan-millennialist – I think it will all pan out in the end!

We get confused when we treat the visions in Revelation as a vision of sequences – as a chronology of the 'end times', in which John offers us a timetable of the (to him distant) future. This cannot be the case! When John wrote, it was recognised that he was speaking to people he knew and was addressing their situation; the text is full of references to real life in the first century. And no one has ever read this text and said, 'This says nothing to me – it must be about the distant future!' Revelation 22:10 makes this clear; where Daniel has been told to 'seal the words' for a future time (Daniel 12:4), John is told, 'Do *not* seal up the words… because the time is near'. Just as the four horsemen in chapter 6 describe four aspects of disaster in the world and not a sequence of four separate events, and the three sequences of seals, trumpets and bowls describe the world in three different ways, so the seven visions John has in chapters 19—21 ('and I saw…' occurs at the beginning of each at Revelation 19:11, 17, 19; 20:1, 4, 11; 21:1) offer seven different perspectives on the *parousia* of Jesus and what it means.

What does this vision of the thousand years tell us? First, that God truly has won the victory over Satan and the forces of evil. That victory was won on the cross ('They triumphed over him by the blood of the Lamb', Revelation 12:11), and it breaks into the world through lives that honour him, but it will be fully revealed at The End. Second, the saints will be vindicated. Those who have suffered most will take pride of place in the new creation. Third, the earth will not be destroyed but renewed – we will reign on earth with him forever. It is a wonderful vision of hope!

6 A new world coming

We now reach this glorious, luminous, multidimensional picture of the world to come, renewed by the grace and power of God and restored to the glory it was always intended to have. There is much to see here – but first note the direction of travel. The biblical vision of life beyond death is not that we leave our earthly bodies to be with God in heaven, but that heaven comes down to earth and we enjoy the new creation in transformed, resurrection bodies (1 Corinthians 15:42–44). God's presence has been in the temple, in the cube-shaped Holy of Holies (1 Kings 6:20) – but now the whole city is a giant cube (v. 16), covering all the known world. If it was centred on Patmos, it would reach from Rome in the west to Jerusalem in the east. This space is occupied both by the holy presence of God and by his people, who enjoy the intimacy of a divine marriage (Revelation 19:9; 21:9).

The city is not the place where God's people dwell – it *is* the people. The details of what the city is like describe God's people as they will be, perfected by his love. It has great, high walls (v. 12), in the ancient world a sign of security and protection. This is the ultimate safe space. It has gates on all four sides (v. 13); people are welcomed from every direction. It is a place of both inclusion and exclusion; the gates are never closed (v. 25), yet 'nothing impure will ever enter it' (v. 27) and angels guard the gates to make it so (v. 12). Each gate represents the kingdom of God, the pearl of great price (v. 21; Matthew 13:45–46); the names of the tribes remind us that we find the kingdom in the true Israel of God (v. 12). The city is built upon the apostolic testimony (the foundations, v. 14) and is centred around Father, Son and Holy Spirit – God and the lamb on the throne from which flows the river of the water of life (22:1).

This is what we will be – and by the power of the Spirit what we begin to be now. The gold of the city has been so refined that it is completely transparent; there is no hypocrisy here. And the repeated refrain is the invitation to all to turn from sin and receive the free gift of the offer of life (22:17).

Guidelines

We have discovered two paradoxical things about eschatology, the study of the last things and the end of the world. First, it is more important than we often realise, being near the centre of the gospel and Christian discipleship. Second, it is much more straightforward than we are led to believe; the diverse and complex texts here have a relatively simple core message, though that is expressed in different ways in different contexts, drawing out different implications.

Jesus died, was raised and has ascended to the Father, and one day he will return to complete the work he has begun. There is no 'end times' timetable; there will be no 'signs of the times'. His coming will be like a thief breaking in, like a master returning suddenly from a journey or like lightning striking – all without warning. So to be ready we need to be getting on with the business of living faithfully for him; Martin Luther said that if he knew Jesus was coming tomorrow, he would still collect the rent and plant an apple tree.

The complication comes in the nature of Jesus' death and resurrection, and what it means for the end of the world. The Jews expected, from the promises of the Old Testament, that God would come and set his people free, that this old age of sin and injustice would end and that the new age would start with everything restored. Jesus brought that restoration, and his resurrection signified that the new age had come, God's future hope breaking into the present. But the old age has not yet passed away! We are therefore living in the overlap of the ages – and this is the central reality of Christian discipleship. For anyone who is in Christ, the new creation has come (2 Corinthians 5:17). We have received the end-times gift of God's Spirit, who is transforming us into what we will one day be. As we continue living in this old age of sin, we will experience trials and tribulations (John 16:33; Revelation 1:9) – but we live in hope of the world to come, energised by the foretaste of the future we already know.

FURTHER READING

R.T. France, *The Gospel of Matthew (The New International Commentary on the New Testament)* (Eerdmans, 2007).

Ian Paul, *Kingdom, Hope and the End of the World: The 'now' and 'not yet' of eschatology* (Grove Biblical, 2016).

Ian Paul, *How to Read the Book of Revelation* (Grove Biblical, 2003).

Ian Paul, *Revelation (Tyndale New Testament Commentaries)* (IVP, 2018).

Tom Wright, *New Heavens, New Earth: The biblical picture of Christian hope* (Grove Biblical, 1999).

Creation care

Ruth Bancewicz et al.

The recent *Wild Isles* series (BBC, 2023) has been a vivid reminder not just of how beautiful the UK is in the diversity and richness of its wildlife, but how ravaged it has been by climate change, pollution, poor land management, unsustainable fishing practices and habitat destruction. Sir David Attenborough reminds the viewer at regular intervals that, with under 50% of our biodiversity left, the UK is in the bottom 10% of countries worldwide for conservation.

The biblical story is a vivid retelling of this dynamic: of humankind having been called to care for creation but instead acting out of selfishness to cause destruction. There is a call to lament, but not despair. These notes take the reader through that drama, from the wonder and beauty of creation, through ruination and grief, to strength for today and hope for the future. The next two weeks will take you deeper into a set of passages from both Old and New Testaments, including some that are often used in the context of this topic and others that are not.

These notes have been written by a diverse group of participants from the UK, Peru and Sri Lanka. They include representatives of the Faraday Institute for Science and Religion, The John Ray Initiative, A Rocha and Tearfund. Very grateful thanks go to members of the latter three organisations who helped recruit writers for this series.

Our ultimate aim is to link the latest science with up-to-date theology and biblical scholarship, helping you navigate this important and at times difficult field. Our hope is that we will challenge and inspire you in your journey of creation care.

Unless otherwise stated, Bible quotations are taken from the NRSV.

1 Wonders of creation

Ruth Bancewicz, church engagement director,
The Faraday Institute for Science and Religion

Job 38:39—39:30

This first speech of God's in response to Job and his friends offers us a unique glimpse of the created order. Job is forced to move beyond his own descriptive view of the cosmos (9:4–10) to think more deeply about his place in the world. He is 'privy to a God's-eye view of creation in all its beauty, in all its wildness', a 'sole passenger on this grand tour of the cosmos' (Schifferdecker, 2008).

What follows reveals a world within a world – largely away from human interference – that is complex, ordered, powerful, beautiful and not always comfortable. The animals are paired based on qualities they share: the lion and raven as predators, the herbivorous wild goat and hind, the wild ass and ox as un-domesticable varieties of domestic animals, the fearless ostrich and war horse, and finally the raptors – the hawk and eagle (or vulture). These animals are part of God's kingdom because they are under his eye, receive his help and obey his commands.

For the church fathers, these animals had symbolic or allegorical meanings. For example, the wild ass is a reminder that although some animals can become domesticated, we cannot control everything in creation. In addition to control, there is the question of understanding. We may know more about the mechanisms of flight today, but that's not the point of this passage. No matter how much we learn, any scientist knows that there is always more to discover about the complexity and wonder of the living world. The only one who knows everything about everything is God. This lack of knowledge needn't shut down our scientific exploration of creation but can fuel our search for greater insight into the things God has made and commanded us to tend and keep.

Previously, Job and his friends addressed God as 'El Shaddai,' meaning God Almighty, which could be used to refer to other gods in the surrounding culture. But in this section 'Yahweh', or the Lord, is used: the name God gave himself when speaking to Moses. This personal God is confronting Job with the majesty of creation, giving him the opportunity to be shocked into the silence of awe, but also to find his place in it as a creature with a calling.

2 Till and keep

Dave Bookless, director of theology, A Rocha International

Genesis 1:24–31; 2:7–17

No part of the Bible has generated more contested interpretation than Genesis 1—3. The twin accounts of creation (1:1–2:4a and 2:4b–25) and the entrance of sin into God's good creation (3:1–24) touch on issues including cosmic origins, human nature, gender and sexuality, good and evil, divine purpose and the nature of biblical literature. Here we will limit ourselves to the question, 'What are humans for?', the issue of biblical anthropology.

The phrase 'image of God' (1:26–27) appears in the Hebrew Bible only here and briefly in Genesis 5:1–3 and 9:6. Despite the silence of the rest of the Old Testament, it has been a hugely influential phrase. Arguably, it has inspired the secular concept of human rights, whereby all people, regardless of difference, are of equal value. There have been three broad theological interpretations concerning 'image of God' in humanity: *substantive* (a unique God-given capacity, such as reason, will or conscience), *relational* (the human capacity for relationship with God) and *functional* (a task God gives to humanity). Today, most biblical scholars take the functional view, based on parallels from other ancient Near Eastern religions and the actual context of Genesis 1, where 'image of God' is related to the task of having 'dominion' over the earth and its creatures. To put it simply, bearing God's image is a job description involving delegated responsibility to reflect God's intentions towards creation.

Genesis 2:7 gives a very different, but complementary, perspective on what it means to be human. Rather than exalted as the image of God, humans (*Adam*) are formed from the dust of the ground (*Adamah*). Biologically, this is obvious. We are carbon-based life-forms related to all other earth creatures. Theologically, this is crucial too. We cannot separate ourselves from nature. We are called to reflect God's image among, not above, our fellow creatures.

That brings us to 2:15–17, where God places the first human in the garden to 'till it and keep it'. The words 'till' (*abad*) and 'keep' (*shamar*) cover both agricultural cultivation and the priestly task of serving and guarding in God's temple. This, in essence, is our job description, our first great commission. Creation is a temple to God's glory and we are placed within it to reflect God's image on behalf of our fellow creatures. We glorify God by enabling the flourishing and fruitfulness of God's earth. That, in Genesis 1—2, is what humans are for!

3 Broken relationships

Robert White, emeritus director,
The Faraday Institute for Science and Religion

Genesis 3:16–24; 4:1–16

When Adam and Eve rebelled against God by disobeying him, they set the pattern for all humanity. The consequences were immediate. The breakdown of harmonious relations between humans and God spread to alienation from the created order. This in turn led to disruption in interpersonal relationships, culminating in the first murder recorded in the Bible. Although the general consequences of sin for both Adam and Eve were similar, God pronounced sentences specific to each.

The woman's 'wages of sin' relate to her roles as mother and wife (3:16). Her pains in childbirth were exacerbated. Despite the suffering involved, humans retained the blessing and power of procreation God had given them. But as with all sin, the good that God had brought forth was marred. Sin caused Eve's relationship to Adam to be disrupted, bringing male tyranny and domination into what had been a loving partnership.

For the man, the consequences of putting himself first instead of God were that his relationship to the very ground from which his crops came was cursed. Instead of joyful work in the garden, it became painful toil and a struggle to produce food (3:17–19). The change was not in the nature of the earth and plants themselves, but in the insatiable greed and self-centredness of humans, which pollutes and destroys the earth on which we depend. As we see clearly with climate change and the unprecedented (in human history) rate of species extinctions, we are quite literally turning a garden into a desert.

Lastly, Cain murdered his younger brother Abel. Abel had pleased God by sacrificing the firstborn of his flocks (4:4). Cain had brought some of his crops (4:3), but God wasn't pleased with that. We are not told why; maybe Cain didn't give sacrificially. But it made Cain angry enough to kill, despite God trying to reason with him (4:5–8). Cain's real motive seems to be that he thought he could buy God's favour, and he could not bear the idea of the sovereign God choosing to recognise his brother's faith. Cain was thrown out of his home and family, but even in his wandering God showed mercy by preventing anyone killing him (4:13–15). Likewise, God shows us mercy in our sinfulness, culminating in the sacrifice of his own Son to restore us to relationship with himself.

4 Broken world

Vinoth Ramachandra, secretary for dialogue and social engagement, IFES

Isaiah 24:1–23

With a cluster of vivid poetic images, Isaiah 24 laments the groaning of the earth under the weight of cosmic evil. The Hebrew people never thought of the world as an autonomous, self-sustaining life system ('nature') but, rather, as a *creation* dependent moment by moment on the faithfulness of Yahweh, its creator. Human wickedness, springing from the rejection of Yahweh's moral norms and the Adamic covenant (v. 5), devastates the planet and destroys social life (vv. 7–13), since human well-being and the integrity of the fragile ecological system of the food chain are intimately connected. The fecundity of the earth is disrupted. It is as if the ordered creation itself is being undone, returning to the primeval chaos (v. 10).

This could read easily as a litany of environmental ills culled from our daily news media: military conflicts that scorch the earth; the large-scale plundering of natural resources; the destruction of ecosystems that lead to the rapid extinction of fauna and flora; uncontrolled greenhouse emissions that intensify droughts and floods and wreak havoc on weather patterns.

In a move typical of prophetic imagination, Isaiah sees such human-induced planetary chaos as a harbinger of Yahweh's own approaching judgement. Yahweh has an appointed day when he will punish the kings of the earth and the cosmic powers that uphold an idolatrous world system (v. 21). The earth will be 'laid waste', made utterly desolate (vv. 1, 3). All alike will suffer, irrespective of social position or function (v. 2). Such indiscriminate judgement raises awkward questions, then and now. Why does the oppressed suffer along with the oppressor? It seems that we, as a result of our social nature, are 'all in it together'.

However, when the world system is judged, those who have no stake in its perpetuation will rejoice and give praise to Yahweh (vv. 14–16a). We are not told who 'they' are, but they are clearly the faithful community of Yahweh who await his intervention. They come not from the centres of political and economic power, but from all over the world, including the remote 'coastlands of the sea' (v. 15). For them, the judgement on a cruel and exploitative world order is good news. It paves the way for a new regime of global governance under Yahweh (v. 23), the dawn of a renewed creation.

5 The earth mourns

Roger Abbott, senior research associate,
The Faraday Institute for Science and Religion

Isaiah 24:4–10 (ESV)

Recently, I interviewed two botanical scientists at Kew Gardens. One is a Christian and the other avowedly not, yet they both expressed the same response to the conclusions of their research: lament. One shared with me that while working in the Brazilian Atlantic Forest, one of the richest ecosystems in the world, she found that just a single teaspoonful of soil contained around 1,800 plant species – the same number as we have in the whole of the UK. The other shared his experience with the ash dieback pandemic, a disease that is devastating the world's ash trees. The cause? Human irresponsibility in transporting trees carrying pests into gardens around the world.

The interaction between humans and the natural environment ('the earth') is a serious one when viewed from the perspective of God's holiness and human irresponsibility. Such appalling creation abuse should break our hearts like it did Isaiah's, like it does God's, and, in anthropomorphic terms, like it does the 'earth' (v. 4). Surely there can be only one appropriate response: lament, repentance and trust in the same Saviour the whole of creation is looking for with outstretched neck to bring redemption at the last (Romans 8:19–23).

Isaiah says the earth 'mourns' (v. 4) – it is languishing, not flourishing, a lamentable shadow of what it was created to be. In fact, 'the earth lies defiled' (v. 5). But who is *responsible* for this defilement? Not the Creator, but the whole of 'earth's inhabitants' are responsible (vv. 5–6). By flouting the principles of the earth's care, those charged with that task have in fact abused it. Today, we speak of the raping of the earth. This passage is a vivid description of the horrific abuse carried out upon creation by its human carers. As the following verses make clear, such creation abuse will inevitably make lives miserable and empty (v.v. 6–9) as the 'earth' is left lying in misery and shame, as if 'cursed.' But the reality is that the 'earth' is innocent; it is her shameless carers who have committed the horrendous evil. This is why the attitude and practice of lament are the only appropriate stances we humans should adopt, all the more so as the ravages of human-induced climate change are accelerating misery in a mourning earth.

6 God's commitment

Margot Hodson, director of theology and education,
The John Ray Initiative

Genesis 9:1–17

In 2022 the UK parliament passed the Animal Welfare (Sentience) Act. This acknowledged that animals experience emotions and feel pain. Moreover, it goes beyond vertebrates, and animals such as lobsters and octopuses now have some welfare protection for the first time. Paradoxically, the law does not outlaw existing practices, so lobsters can still be boiled alive, despite evidence that they experience pain and distress.

Genesis begins by portraying a harmonious relationship between humans and animals, but the breakdown in relationships resulting from the fall in Genesis 3 left animals vulnerable to human ill-treatment. By the time of Noah, animals had become fearful of humans. The flood brings a fresh start, and God resets the relationships between humans and the rest of his creation. God sets limits. Humans are now allowed to eat animals but must slaughter them, draining out the life-giving blood. Ancient Hebrews believed that the soul (*nephesh*) resided in the blood of a creature. Since it was breathed into them by God, it should be drained back to the ground and not consumed. Furthermore, God would demand a reckoning for not keeping this commandment and for shedding human blood.

The covenant with Noah is a universal covenant made between God, humans and animals. It is interesting that, when the early Jewish Christians wrote to the new Gentile believers (Acts 15), they quoted from this covenant. Gentiles had never been required to follow Mosaic laws, but these Noachian laws were seen as universal.

Alongside these limits, God places a limit on himself. When the rainbow appears he will remember the covenant. So this covenant is making the best of circumstances that are not ideal. The world is no longer perfect, but God loves his creation and wants us to partner with him in its care. God blesses Noah and encourages him to be fruitful and multiply. The word 'fill' (*mala*) could also mean 'replenish'. This repeats the command in Genesis 1:28, but omits the command to 'subdue'. Maybe humans had wrongly taken that command as freedom to damage and destroy? Today, the protection of the biodiversity of this planet is in our hands. Let us work with God and be guided by him in our care for creation, to replenish and not harm.

Guidelines

This week's passages have focused on God's incredible creation, our task of tending and keeping it and how we have failed in that task. The consequences of our selfishness are the despoiling of creation, human hardship and lament. But we are not left there. God remains committed to his creation.

How often does teaching on creation care happen in your own church? If you are responsible for the preaching plan, can you address this topic on several Sundays each year? If you are not a church leader, can you make some constructive suggestions to those in leadership? It's hopefully apparent to any trained clergy person how to teach on the doctrine of creation, fall and redemption with reference to creation care. If you're looking for guidance, however, the theologian Chris Wright has included this topic in several of his wide-ranging books on biblical themes (see also further reading).

For exploring more specialist issues, such as climate change or biodiversity, resources for churches are listed in the further reading. It's also worth thinking about how we can include science in our teaching and preaching. How many ways can you think of doing this? A list is given below, but it is not comprehensive!

- Stories of scientists or scientific discoveries that invoke awe, wonder and worship.
- Science as a tool to deepen understanding or impact of a biblical passage.
- Scientific stories as parables to convey a biblical message.
- Scientific stories that convey biblical wisdom (e.g. Proverbs 30:25–28).
- Using science to motivate practical action.
- Scientists who share their own stories of faith and science in action.

How many of these techniques can you use in your church (with help from any scientists or science-oriented people in your congregation)?

1 Creation is still good

Martin Hodson, principal tutor of Christian rural and environmental studies, The John Ray Initiative

Psalm 8

As a scientist I have been privileged to have seen and discovered some things that nobody else ever saw or knew about before. For many years, I used electron microscopes to look at plant cells and tissues at very high magnification. I really was seeing some of the work of God's fingers, and I still feel amazingly blessed to have had those opportunities. If I was looking at the micro-scale, then Psalm 8 definitely begins at the macro-scale. While I was investigating plant ultrastructure, the psalm first considers the heavens, the stars and the moon, before moving on to mammals, birds and fish.

Psalm 8 is short, but expansive, taking in the whole created order. David's psalm is a song of praise bookended by 'O Lord, our Sovereign, how majestic is your name in all the earth!' It is clearly related to the creation narratives in Genesis 1 and 2, in which creation is seen as 'good'. But as we know, Genesis 3 soon follows, where human sin causes the damaging of relationships between God, humans and the environment.

Throughout history some have thought that the fall so corrupted the earth that it became bad or evil. This has led people to believe that the only way out from this degraded world is to escape to some sort of perfect higher spiritual realm. This kind of dualistic thinking, which still exists in some parts of the church today, has been very harmful. If the creation is evil, there is no point in caring for it. If all our focus is on attaining a higher spiritual existence, then we will hardly show any concern for the environment.

But look again at Psalm 8. There is no indication at all that the created order is bad or evil. This psalm was written well after the fall, and David would have been well aware of Genesis 3. In fact, if we take the whole Bible into account there is no sign that the creation itself is bad. Other psalms confirm this. For instance, Psalm 24:1 has: 'The earth is the Lord's and all that is in it, the world, and those who live in it.' It may be marred by human sin, but the creation still belongs to God and is basically good – at both the micro- and macro-scales!

2 Sustainer

Hannah Gray, programme manager, WaterAid

Psalm 147

Psalm 147 is a song of praise to God for his provision and power, probably written when the Israelites returned to Jerusalem following their exile in Babylon. It contains jubilant stanzas of celebration that God has provided security and peace for his people, who had been through tough times (vv. 2–3), and abundant provision for their physical needs in their own land (v. 14). It is a resounding affirmation that Yahweh, not the gods of Babylon, is sovereign over everything. The God of Zion orchestrates the weather to make the grass grow, providing sustenance for livestock and people (vv. 7–9, 14). It is his word that causes both frost and thaw (vv. 15–18). His sustenance even extends to the ravens (v. 9), which were regarded with contempt (Leviticus 11:13–15).

God has created self-sustaining systems which govern the functioning of our planet, from the weather and oceanic currents to nutrient cycles and ecosystems. God doesn't need to operate these directly like a puppet master, yet he is always there, behind the scenes, sustaining them all. Instinctively, we inhale a blend of gases required by our body to breathe, and we consume water and food that has the nutrition required for movement. Our everyday, routine lives are totally reliant on this perfectly balanced and exquisitely designed physical world. And yet our collective actions are now changing the carefully calibrated atmosphere and degrading productive soils, increasing inequality, poverty and vulnerability.

If we believe God sustains life, what does that mean for people who love God and follow Jesus? The Israelites were encouraged to tend their farms responsibly, not harvesting the edges of the fields and allowing gleaning by the poor (Leviticus 23:22), having fallow years for the land to rest and the wild animals to eat (Leviticus 25:1–7), keeping land in good condition for future generations. We also should live sustainably on the earth, recognising its planetary limits and not taking more than our share – we must consider what else depends on the earth for survival and flourishing. God's sustenance is not limitless; we cannot greedily draw down on nature's bounty without causing injustice to someone or something, now or in the future.

Let us praise God for his sustaining role in creation and pray for wisdom to live sustainably in this precious world we call home. Let us become active participants in God's sustenance for people and planet.

3 Hope for today

Jo Swinney, head of communications, A Rocha International

1 Corinthians 1:18–31

Back in the first decades after Jesus' time on earth, human-caused environmental catastrophe was still a long way over the horizon. But this extract from Paul's letter to the church in Corinth points to the same bedrock of hope on which we can stand today, because the pertinent question remains: who is the Saviour? We are all perishing: who can save us?

The Corinthian church was rather enamoured of the concept of *Sophia*, wisdom. By referring to 'wisdom' or 'the wise' 13 times in these few lines, Paul is definitely making a point! Their fixation was influenced by two religious influences in Corinth: Isis, described by Plutarch as 'a goddess exceptionally wise and a lover of wisdom,' and the cult of Mithras, known for its mysterious initiation tests and multi-levelled holiness. The problem was that seeking this kind of wisdom inevitably led to pride and the dangerous idea that you could, by your own wisdom, save yourself.

The dominant narrative around biodiversity loss and climate change in the UK today is that, yes, the outlook is bleak, but we will save the planet by inventing new technologies, changing our lifestyles and adapting to new conditions. While on the face of things this seems an optimistic and empowering stance, it gives us a crushing weight of responsibility. If the world's problems seem overwhelming, that is because they are if you are a human.

Paul can be harsh when the occasion calls for it. Here, he sharpens his needle and goes about bursting the Corinthians' bubble. By human standards they are rather foolish, he says. Remember that most of you have no social status or influence. You are weak, lowly and despised (vv. 26–28). And doesn't that sound like most church congregations all these centuries later?

But in the gloriously upside-down kingdom of God, these are the very people best placed to demonstrate the power, strength and wisdom of Jesus Christ. Paul's timely word for us today is that it is not on us to save the world. We can and must do all we can to serve, protect and restore the earth. But the world has a Saviour, who created it, sustains it and has pledged eternal fidelity to it.

Taking positive action demonstrates hope. It says loud and clear that we believe salvation is not only possible, but that it is also the outcome we expect and that with God's help, it will come to pass.

4 Hope for the future

Rodney Holder, former course director,
The Faraday Institute for Science and Religion

The idea that the creation (*ktisis*), meaning here the natural world apart from humans, was 'subjected to futility' would seem *prima facie* to take us back to the story of Adam and Eve in the garden (Genesis 3). As a result of their sin the ground is cursed and brings up thorns and thistles, the pangs of childbirth are increased, and the husband rules the wife. We know that there has been no sudden change in the laws of nature in the 4½ billion years of the earth's history, so it seems to me better to interpret this as the way humans in general relate to nature in the light of our sin. The Hebrew word *adam* means 'man', so Adam in the story may be taken symbolically to mean 'Everyman'.

Human sin corrupts all our relationships: first and foremost our relationship with God, then with each other and with the natural world. Today's passage relates strongly to the 'Isaiah apocalypse' of Isaiah 24—27, where we read that God is about to lay waste the earth. The earth lies polluted because its inhabitants have 'broken the everlasting covenant', and so 'a curse devours the earth' (Isaiah 24:5–6).

The good news is that this is not the end of the story. There is hope; as we say at funeral services, 'sure and certain hope of the resurrection to eternal life'. In Isaiah 25 we read that God will 'swallow up death forever' and 'wipe away tears from all faces' (v. 8). Today's passage is similar. Both us and creation with its labour pains are groaning as we await 'the redemption of our bodies' (v. 23). What we look forward to is our own resurrection and the renewal of the whole created physical world.

We live in the 'now and not yet'. We are redeemed but await the redemption of our bodies. As Dietrich Bonhoeffer observed, our resurrection hope does not detach us from the world; it drives us back into it. We spread the good news of relationship with God restored through Christ to those who don't know it. We must also treat the natural world as we should. Evidence of the effect of human sin on creation is more evident now that at any time in human history. May our hope for the future drive us to action now to save the climate and protect threatened species.

5 Release from eco-anxiety

Anne Scott, lay church-planting pioneer and
Outdoor Worship network leader

Psalm 139

A legitimate response to the climate crisis is anxiety. We can feel guilt for having been an active participant in a society which has caused so much damage, worry for future generations for the world they will inherit or grief for the loss of species which are no longer able to reveal our creator.

Climate anxiety, which the American Psychological Association in 2017 defined as 'a chronic fear of environmental doom', is experienced within our churches as well as general society (Tearfund, 2021).

Climate grief encompasses the range of emotions we experience as we face any major loss: denial, anger, bargaining and depression. Sometimes these emotions hit us hard when we experience the loss of an endangered or extinct species: we grieve the disappearance of a unique expression of creation. Sometimes grief can be a gradual process, akin to watching a loved relative suffer with dementia, and we grieve for each step away from the world we knew. It's a painful process to constantly readjust to life in a new norm.

The psalmist reminds us that God knows us and is familiar with all our ways: made in his image, we feel the pain he feels as he looks at his broken world. We are created to experience his heart of justice and it is right that we are affected when we see what is happening around us. The psalm legitimises the expression of anger, frustration and anxiety to God (vv. 19–23) and joins us in calling for God's justice.

God does not leave us in a place of anxiety, worry, guilt or grief but leads us forwards into his plans (v. 16). As we allow God to search us and test our anxiety (v. 23), those emotions which are unhealthy, and which hinder us, are transformed by our creator's everlasting plans (v. 24).

The all-encompassing presence of God, which is before, behind and above us (v. 5), longs to share his precious thoughts with us: we are encouraged to listen to his voice in the midst of the anxiety and worry (v. 17). We are not meant to carry the pains and the sorrows of the world – Jesus has already done that – but we are reconciled with God to reclaim the creation mandate: to enable all of creation to flourish. With this deep knowledge of God's love for us, we can walk out of our darkness into his light, bringing him our anxiety and allowing him to lead us (v. 24).

6 Freedom to live

Steve W. Privat-Perez, coordinator of 'Que Agro con mi Vida' and climate justice activist

Romans 6

This passage is about the sanctification of the believer in Christ. In that sense, Paul is trying to explain to the Christians in Rome the importance of living a holy life separated from sin, but it also has important implications for our relationship with creation.

Paul explains that our union with Christ in his death and resurrection means that our old sinful nature has been crucified with him. We are no longer bound to remain slaves to sin, but are now free to live a righteous life pleasing to God.

This freedom applies not only to our relationship with God, but also with creation. As Christians, we must be aware of our responsibility to care for the earth and all the creatures that inhabit it. This means that our sanctified life can have a positive impact not only on our own life, but also on creation. If we live a righteous life and respect nature, we can help to heal the damage that humanity has caused to the environment.

However, Paul also recognises that sanctification is not something that happens automatically once someone is converted in faith. Instead, it is an ongoing process that requires the believer to submit daily to the Holy Spirit and renounce his or her old sinful nature. This may include renouncing practices that harm the environment, such as excessive energy use and irresponsible exploitation of natural resources, among others. We can seek the Spirit's guidance on how we can be more aware of our ecological footprint and how we can be better stewards of our God-given creation.

Finally, the passage speaks of the ultimate reward of living a sanctified life: eternal life. But this reward applies not only to our life after death, but also to our life here. If we live a righteous life and respect God's creation, we can experience the reward of a healthier and more sustainable life on earth. Therefore, we should renounce excessive consumption of plastic, support environmental movements in their struggles and balance our diets, among other measures. If we do so, we can experience the reward of a healthier and more sustainable life on earth, because we will be generating a community spirit among God's creatures, as it was in the beginning.

Guidelines

Another feature of the BBC documentary *Wild Isles* was to showcase some conservation efforts. For example, it featured rewilding on the Knepp estate that resulted in Purple Emperor butterflies returning. There was also mention of the impact of a no-fishing zone in a bay of the Isle of Arran. Sometimes simply leaving creation alone can let it recover. At other times more active intervention is used. The Knepp rewilding project, for example, carried out re-seeding of wild meadow flowers on some of its land.

We don't all have to be involved in such large-scale conservation efforts, but we can all do something. What steps, big or small, can you and your church take to care for creation in the coming year?

- Project Drawdown (**drawdown.org/solutions/table-of-solutions**) lists the most effective actions to mitigate climate change, with reducing food waste and plant-rich diets coming top of the list. Do any of the ideas listed inspire you to try something new in your own home?
- Take some time to think through the resources your church already has and the activities it carries out. Identify one creation-care action that you could try or suggest. If you need inspiration, explore the websites in the further reading section.

FURTHER READING

Jo Swinney and Miranda Harris, *A Place at The Table: Faith, hope and hospitality* (Hodder and Stoughton, 2022).

Martin and Margot Hodson, *Green Reflections: Biblical inspiration for sustainable living* (BRF, 2021).

Hannah Malcolm (ed.), *Words for a Dying World: Stories of grief and courage from the global church* (SCM, 2020).

Hilary Marlow, *The Earth Is the Lord's: A biblical response to environmental issues* (Grove Books, 2008).

Kathryn Schifferdecker, *Out of the Whirlwind: Creation theology in the book of Job* (Harvard University Press, 2008).

Doxecology: songs and resources for churches (**resoundworship.org/projects/doxecology**).

Tearfund (2021), 'Burning down the house: how the church could lose young people over climate inaction' (**weare.tearfund.org/burning-down-the-house**).

The Faraday Institute for Science and Religion (**faraday.cam.ac.uk**).

A Rocha UK (**arocha.org.uk**).

The John Ray Initiative (**jri.org.uk**).

SHARING OUR VISION – MAKING A GIFT

I would like to make a donation to support BRF Ministries.
Please use my gift for:

☐ Where it is most needed ☐ Anna Chaplaincy ☐ Living Faith

☐ Messy Church ☐ Parenting for Faith

Title	First name/initials	Surname	
Address			
			Postcode
Email			
Telephone			
Signature			Date

Our ministry is only possible because of the generous support of individuals, churches, trusts and gifts in wills.

Please treat as Gift Aid donations all qualifying gifts of money made (*tick all that apply*) *giftaid it*

☐ today, ☐ in the past four years, ☐ and in the future.

I am a UK taxpayer and understand that if I pay less Income Tax and/or Capital Gains Tax in the current tax year than the amount of Gift Aid claimed on all my donations, it is my responsibility to pay any difference.

☐ My donation does not qualify for Gift Aid.

Please notify BRF Ministries if you want to cancel this Gift Aid declaration, change your name or home address, or no longer pay sufficient tax on your income and/or capital gains.

You can also give online at **brf.org.uk/donate**, which reduces our administration costs, making your donation go further.

Please complete other side of form

SHARING OUR VISION – MAKING A GIFT

Please accept my gift of:

☐ £2 ☐ £5 ☐ £10 ☐ £20 Other £ [　　　]

by (*delete as appropriate*):

☐ Cheque/Charity Voucher payable to 'BRF'

☐ MasterCard/Visa/Debit card/Charity card

Name on card

Card no. [ ][ ][ ][ ] [ ][ ][ ][ ] [ ][ ][ ][ ] [ ][ ][ ][ ] [ ][ ][ ][ ]

Expires end [M][M] [Y][Y] Security code* [ ][ ][ ] *Last 3 digits on the reverse of the card

Signature | Date

☐ I would like to leave a gift to BRF Ministries in my will.
Please send me further information.

☐ I would like to find out about giving a regular gift to BRF Ministries.

For help or advice regarding making a gift, please contact
our fundraising team +44 (0)1865 462305

Your privacy

We will use your personal data to process this transaction.
From time to time we may send you information about
the work of BRF Ministries that we think may be of
interest to you. Our privacy policy is available at
brf.org.uk/privacy. Please contact us if you wish to
discuss your mailing preferences.

Registered with

FUNDRAISING
REGULATOR

● Please complete other side of form

Please return this form to 'Freepost BRF'
No other address information or stamp is needed

Bible Reading Fellowship is a charity (233280) and company limited by guarantee (301324),
registered in England and Wales

GL0224

Overleaf… Guidelines forthcoming issue | Author profile |
Recommended reading | Order and subscription forms

Guidelines forthcoming issue

The next issue of *Guidelines* continues to guide and nourish you. I hope that you will join us for it. Here is a taster of what to expect.

Bill Goodman reaches the end of his epic series on the book of Psalms in the next issue. We have looked at each of the books of the Psalms, and will now conclude with Book V. Andrew Boakye will also conclude his series on Galatians, taking us from chapter 3 to the end of the book. Isabelle Hamley takes up the mantle for our gospel series, guiding us on 'a journey in discipleship' as we look at Luke 9—16.

Our Old Testament series for this issue are Esther, written by former *Guidelines* editor Helen Payner, and Joshua, written by Leoné Martin. Neither make particularly comfortable reading, but our hope is that both will provide you with a deeper understanding of who God is.

In the New Testament, George Wieland will help us with the short books of Titus and Philemon. Meanwhile, Rachel Tranter looks at the use of the Old Testament in the New Testament, with examples from Matthew, Ephesians and Revelation. These different types of uses help us to contextualise the Old Testament and understand how the New Testament writers saw the scriptures in light of Jesus' life, death and resurrection.

As we journey into Advent, we are in good company. David Spriggs invites us to think about forgiveness, while Cally Hammond reflects on how, where and when we find Jesus in the world. Siobhán Jolley considers Mary Magdalene and whether she was mad, bad and dangerous to know – or something else entirely? Finally, Elizabeth Dodd invites us to ponder the poetry of the Magnificat: a song of victory, a prophetic poem and a hymn of praise.

As we journey through the final section of the year towards our Advent celebrations, we hope that these notes continue to draw you closer to the love of God expressed through Jesus.

What the Bible means to me: Andrew Boakye

 As a British taxpayer, HM Revenue and Customs has never asked me about my life – who I am, what I value, my sense of purpose or my life goals. There is a reason for this: no one in HMRC is interested! They offer me rules, regulations and protocols, but they do not seek a relationship with me. When I first met my wife of 24 years, we were deeply interested in the intimate details of one another's lives. We invited one another into our respective stories because what we wanted was a relationship – not a wooden, pedestrian, academic liaison. I see in the background of this contrast a most important dictum – when we seek a relationship, we invite people into our story.

I muse over the Christian sacred texts daily because I seek a relationship; to my deep-rooted joy, I discovered that the God who created everything had been seeking a relationship long before the thought ever entered a human mind. I discovered that the creator God was inviting me into his story. This is the enigmatic story of creation and the fall, of the election of Israel, of the hopes of Israel bearing down on the Messiah, the in-breaking of God's kingdom and the coming of God's Spirit, the creation of communities built around the resurrection of the Messiah and the awaited return of the Messiah to earth.

This was not and is not an abstract or distant narrative, but one which beckons humanity into its very core. What began as his story became our story, one in which the God who reigns through Christ in the power of his Spirit is the central character and humanity is the rest of the cast. This is a story in which I have a pivotal role to play, and understanding that role is a journey and not a destination. Regularly immersing myself in the Bible not only tells me about the nature, meaning and purpose of the story; it also teaches me about my intrinsic value in the eyes of the central character. It shapes and informs my understanding of the human condition and of what it means to experience the world, clarifying my vision of reality, helping me navigate my innermost intuitions and demonstrating how the most pristine of virtues meet together in the person of Jesus in a way that is simultaneously supernatural and human. Precisely because the Bible is so strange and yet so familiar, so powerful and yet so tender, oftentimes so confusing and yet simultaneously the source of all clarity, so beautiful and yet so terrifying, so divine and yet so completely human – it so perfectly speaks into life now and life to come.

Recommended reading

On the way to work this morning, what were you thinking about? If you have a long commute, maybe you
had more thinking time than if you work from home.
Whatever length your journey, do you look forward to
beginning your working day? Does your work give you
a sense of purpose? How do you feel when work serves
up difficulties and problems? How do we work well?
Is there a God, and might God have something to say
about the way we work?

Weaving together biblical perspectives with aca-
demic research and his own experiences of working in different settings,
Chris Gillies lays the theological foundation for work, moves on to examin-
ing biblical role models from both Old and New Testaments, and concludes
by exploring common issues we wrestle with in our work, from money
matters or managing and leading others to knowing if we're in the right
job or simply doing the right thing.

The following is an edited extract taken from chapter 9, 'How do I know
if I'm in the right job?'.

Oft-quoted scriptures, frequently used in a platitudinous way, can lull us
into a sense that everything's going to be all right. For example, Jeremiah
29:11 (NIV): '"For I know the plans I have for you," declares the Lord, "plans
to prosper you and not to harm you, plans to give you a hope and a future."'
Or Romans 8:28 (NIV): 'And we know that in all things God works for the good
of those who love him, who have been called according to his purpose.' If
God has a plan for our lives, if we're called, why do so many of us encounter
problems along the way? How do we discern what that plan might be? And
if we're working in line with his plan, according to his purpose, is it realistic
to expect all the problems will melt away?

I've learned that God does have a purpose for each of us, and it's not his
heart to deliberately conceal that purpose from us. However, we often fall into
two traps when thinking about these things. First, we assume that God's plan
is going to be detailed and personalised, so we lose sight of the overarching
purpose he has for all humans; and second, we fail to realise that God's plan
is dynamically dependent on our own personal formation – adjusting to our
mistakes and keeping pace with our development. If we're slow to grow, God's

plan will be dynamically matched to our maturity rate, and problem-solving may be an important ingredient in helping us grow.

My grandmother created wool tapestries. Sometimes, when she was working on one of these, she would be working from the back of the tapestry and all I could see would be a jumble of colours, an ugly mess of loose ends, with no discernible picture. When she had worked on it for a while and then turned it over, the beautiful picture became clear. God weaves a pattern from the threads of our lives – including the mistakes and heartaches – to make something beautiful. While he is still weaving, we may not be able to see a discernible picture, but when we look back the design becomes clear.

Søren Kierkegaard said, 'Life can only be understood backwards; but it must be lived forwards.' Sometimes we must fight our way forwards in the dark. Only when we reach eternity will God's purpose and plan become completely clear.

People talk about a calling or vocation. I've found that many young Christians are waiting for such a call, as if God is going to ring them up on their smartphone with a clear message to go and work in a certain place in a specific job. Their eagerness to have their calling confirmed can blind them to many other ways in which God might guide us.

God's primary call to every human being down the generations is to a relationship, not to a job. That relationship is founded upon and made possible by the person of Jesus. As far as God is concerned, that relationship comes first, and therein we find our identity. The vocation coming out of our response to that relationship is secondary. We should not let our job define us too much: that can lead to a disproportionate sense of loss should we have the misfortune to be made redundant or to be dismissed, but more importantly, we can miss our primary identity driver, which is relational.

God commissioned us to look after the planet and to build a flourishing society. His calling on the life of every human being involves work – maybe work that is creative, that brings order where there is chaos, that helps sustain the environment and the planet's natural resources or that provides the goods, services and relationships that society needs to flourish. It is more important to consider how we should go about that work.

To order a copy of this book, please use the order form on page 151 or visit **brfonline.org.uk**

KNOWING
YOU, JESUS
| 365 DEVOTIONAL

*following Jesus through
the gospels in a year*

Tony Horsfall   Mags Duggan   John Ayrton
Jenny Brown   Melinda Hendry   Steve Aisthorpe

This 365-day devotional is a response to the famous prayer of Richard of Chichester 'to see thee more clearly, to love thee more dearly and follow thee more nearly'. In it Tony Horsfall, Mags Duggan, John Ayrton, Jenny Brown, Melinda Hendry and Steve Aisthorpe present a detailed, chronological exploration of the life of Jesus of Nazareth, drawing from all four gospels. As we immerse ourselves in the gospel story, may we not only understand it better but also experience transformation into the likeness of Christ our Saviour.

Knowing You, Jesus: 365 Devotional
Following Jesus through the gospels in a year
Tony Horsfall et al.
978 1 80039 185 7 £19.99
brfonline.org.uk

**Spiritual Growth
in a Time of Change**

Following God in midlife

Tony Horsfall

Our 40s and 50s can be times of change and turbulent emotional transitions as we encounter a range of challenging personal issues. They can also be some of the most important years of our lives in spiritual terms. Tony Horsfall addresses a number of 'midlife' issues – from facing up to the past to renegotiating relationships – and explores how to navigate a spiritual journey through these years, leading to deeper faith and a closer walk with God.

Spiritual Growth in a Time of Change
Following God in midlife
Tony Horsfall
978 1 85746 435 4 £9.99
brfonline.org.uk

Six-session course handbook
Creative arts workshop
Sermon starters
Bible studies
Meditations
Prayer walk

A church's guide
to exploring mortality

Death & Life

Joanna Collicutt
Jo Ind
Victoria Slater
Alison Webster

This research-based book includes all you need to plan and deliver a course enabling people – old or young, healthy or frail – to prepare practically, emotionally and spiritually for their last months on this earth. The course covers six topics: legal practicalities; life stories; funeral planning; physical aspects of dying; spiritual aspects of dying; and the life to come. It also offers a range of materials on the theme of living well in the light of mortality: a creative workshop, sermon starters, Bible studies, meditations and a set of prayer stations which combine to form a prayer walk.

Death and Life
Following Jesus through the gospels in a year
Joanna Collicutt, Jo Ind, Victoria Slater and Alison Webster
978 1 80039 283 0 £19.99
brfonline.org.uk

o order

line: **brfonline.org.uk**
ephone: **+44 (0)1865 319700**
n–Fri 9.30–17.00

Delivery times within the UK are
normally 15 working days. Prices are
correct at the time of going to press
but may change without prior notice.

tle	Price	Qty	Total
n the Way to Work	£9.99		
he Everyday God	£9.99		
nowing You, Jesus	£19.99		
piritual Growth in a Time of Change	£9.99		
eath and Life	£19.99		

POSTAGE AND PACKING CHARGES			
der value	UK	Europe	Rest of world
der £7.00	£2.00		
00–£29.99	£3.00	Available on request	Available on request
0.00 and over	FREE		

Total value of books	
Donation*	
Postage and packing	
Total for this order	

ase complete in BLOCK CAPITALS

** Please complete and return the
Gift Aid declaration on page 141.*

itle _____ First name/initials _____ Surname _____

ddress _____

_____ Postcode _____

cc. No. _____ Telephone _____

mail _____

Method of payment

❑ Cheque (made payable to BRF)   ❑ MasterCard / Visa

ard no. ⬚⬚⬚⬚ ⬚⬚⬚⬚ ⬚⬚⬚⬚ ⬚⬚⬚⬚ ⬚⬚⬚⬚

xpires end ⬚⬚ ⬚⬚   Security code* ⬚⬚⬚   ** Last 3 digits on the
reverse of the card*

will use your personal data to process this order. From time to time we may send you information
out the work of BRF Ministries. Please contact us if you wish to discuss your mailing preferences.
.org.uk/privacy

ase return this form to:

F Ministries, 15 The Chambers, Vineyard, Abingdon OX14 3FE | **enquiries@brf.org.uk**
terms and cancellation information, please visit brfonline.org.uk/terms.

BRF Ministries needs you!

If you're one of our regular *Guidelines* readers, you will know all about the benefits and blessings of regular Bible study and the value of serious daily notes to guide, inform and challenge you.

Here are some recent comments from *Guidelines* readers:

'... very thoughtful and spiritually helpful. [These notes] are speaking to the church as it is today, and therefore to Christians like us who live in today's world.'

'You have assembled an amazingly diverse group of people and their contributions are most certainly thoughtful.'

If you have similarly positive things to say about *Guidelines*, would you be willing to share your experience with others? Could you ask for a brief slot during church notices or write a short piece for your church magazine or website? Do you belong to groups, formal or informal, academic or professional, where you could share your experience of using *Guidelines* and encourage others to try them?

It doesn't need to be complicated: just answering these three questions in what you say or write will get your message across:

- How do *Guidelines* Bible study notes help you grow in knowledge and faith?
- Where, when and how do you use them?
- What would you say to people who haven't yet tried them?

We can supply further information if you need it and would love to hear about it if you do give a talk or write an article.

For more information:

- Email **enquiries@brf.org.uk**
- Telephone BRF Ministries on **+44 (0)1865 319700** Mon–Fri 9.30–17.00
- Write to us at BRF Ministries, 15 The Chambers, Vineyard, Abingdon OX14 3FE

Inspiring people of all ages to grow in Christian faith

BRF Ministries

At BRF Ministries, we long for people of all ages to grow in faith and understanding of the Bible. That's what all our work as a charity is about.

- Our **Living Faith** range of resources helps Christians go deeper in their understanding of scripture, in prayer and in their walk with God. Our conferences and events bring people together to share this journey, while our Holy Habits resources help whole congregations grow together as disciples of Jesus, living out and sharing their faith.

- We also want to make it easier for local churches to engage effectively in ministry and mission – by helping them bring new families into a growing relationship with God through **Messy Church** or by supporting churches as they nurture the spiritual life of older people through **Anna Chaplaincy**.

- Our **Parenting for Faith** team coaches parents and others to raise God-connected children and teens, and enables churches to fully support them.

Do you share our vision?

Though a significant proportion of BRF Ministries' funding is generated through our charitable activities, we are dependent on the generous support of individuals, churches and charitable trusts.

If you share our vision, would you help us to enable even more people of all ages to grow in faith? Your prayers and financial support are vital for the work that we do. You could:

- Support BRF Ministries with a regular donation;
- Support us with a one-off gift;
- Consider leaving a gift to BRF Ministries in your will (see page 154);
- Encourage your church to support BRF Ministries as part of your church's giving to home mission – perhaps focusing on a specific ministry;
- Most important of all, support BRF Ministries with your prayers.

Donate at **brf.org.uk/donate** or use the form on pages 141–42.

Bearing fruit

'Remain in me, as I also remain in you. No branch can bear fruit by itself; it must remain in the vine. Neither can you bear fruit unless you remain in me.'

JOHN 15:4 (NIV)

As a charity, BRF Ministries is always doing a huge assortment of things, from our Anna Chaplaincy team equipping people to minister to older people to our Messy Church team bringing Jesus to families across the world. From our Parenting for Faith ministry reaching parents and church leaders to transform ideas about how to raise God-connected children to our Living Faith resources that span so many different topics to help people to develop their faith journey.

At a glance these activities might seem distant or disparate but a closer look shows the vine from which all our ministries grow. The mission set out by Leslie Mannering over 100 years ago to which we still hold today: inspiring people of all ages to grow in faith. God is at the heart of all that we do and we are hugely thankful for all the fruits we have born through this work over the last century and more.

We want to keep building on this work, adapting, growing and finding even more glorious ways for people to grow in their faith while still remaining rooted to our mission.

This work would not be possible without kind donations from individuals, charitable trusts and gifts in wills. If you would like to support us now and in the future you can become a Friend of BRF Ministries by making a monthly gift of £2 a month or more – we thank you for your friendship.

Judith Moore
Fundraising development officer

Find out more at **brf.org.uk/donate** or get in touch with us on **01235 462305** or via **giving@brf.org.uk**.

Give. Pray. Get involved.
brf.org.uk

Please note our new subscription rates, current until 30 April 2025:

Individual subscriptions
covering 3 issues for under 5 copies, payable in advance
(including postage & packing):

	UK	Europe	Rest of world
Guidelines 1-year subscription	£19.50	£26.85	£30.75
Guidelines 3-year subscription (9 issues)	£57.60	N/A	N/A

Group subscriptions
covering 3 issues for 5 copies or more, sent to one UK address (post free):

Guidelines 1-year subscription	£14.97 per set of 3 issues p.a.

Please note that the annual billing period for group subscriptions runs from
1 May to 30 April.

Overseas group subscription rates
Available on request. Please email enquiries@brf.org.uk.

Copies may also be obtained from Christian bookshops:

Guidelines	£4.99 per copy

All our Bible reading notes can be ordered online
by visiting **brfonline.org.uk/subscriptions**

All our Bible reading notes can be ordered online by visiting
brfonline.org.uk/subscriptions

Title .... First name/initials .... Surname ....

Address ....

.... Postcode ....

Telephone .... Email ....

Please send *Guidelines* beginning with the September 2024 / January 2025 /
May 2025 issue (*delete as appropriate*):

(*please tick box*)	UK	Europe	Rest of world
Guidelines 1-year subscription	☐ £19.50	☐ £26.85	☐ £30.75
Guidelines 3-year subscription	☐ £57.60	N/A	N/A

Optional donation to support the work of BRF Ministries £ ....

Total enclosed £ .... (cheques should be made payable to 'BRF')

Please complete and return the Gift Aid declaration on page 143 to make your
donation even more valuable to us.

Please charge my MasterCard / Visa with £ ....

Card no. ☐☐☐☐ ☐☐☐☐ ☐☐☐☐ ☐☐☐☐

Expires end ☐M ☐M ☐Y ☐Y Security code ☐☐☐ Last 3 digits on the reverse of the card

To set up a Direct Debit, please complete the Direct Debit instruction on page 159.

We will use your personal data to process this order. From time to time we may send you
information about the work of BRF Ministries. Please contact us if you wish to discuss your mailing
preferences **brf.org.uk/privacy**

Please return this form with the appropriate payment to:
BRF Ministries, 15 The Chambers, Vineyard, Abingdon OX14 3FE
For terms and cancellation information, please visit **brfonline.org.uk/terms**.

BRF

Bible Reading Fellowship is a charity (233280) and company limited by guarantee (301324),
registered in England and Wales

GUIDELINES GIFT SUBSCRIPTION FORM

☐ I would like to give a gift subscription (please provide both names and addresses):

Title _____ First name/initials _____ Surname _____

Address _____

_____ Postcode _____

Telephone _____ Email _____

Gift subscription name _____

Gift subscription address _____

_____ Postcode _____

Gift message (20 words max. or include your own gift card):

_____

_____

Please send *Guidelines* beginning with the September 2024 / January 2025 / May 2025 issue *(delete as appropriate)*:

(please tick box)

	UK	Europe	Rest of world
Guidelines 1-year subscription	☐ £19.50	☐ £26.85	☐ £30.75
Guidelines 3-year subscription	☐ £57.60	N/A	N/A

Optional donation to support the work of BRF Ministries £ _____

Total enclosed £ _____ (cheques should be made payable to 'BRF')

Please complete and return the Gift Aid declaration on page 143 to make your donation even more valuable to us.

Please charge my MasterCard / Visa with £ _____

Card no. ☐☐☐☐ ☐☐☐☐ ☐☐☐☐ ☐☐☐☐

Expires end ☐M☐M ☐Y☐Y   Security code ☐☐☐   Last 3 digits on the reverse of the card

To set up a Direct Debit, please complete the Direct Debit instruction on page 159.

We will use your personal data to process this order. From time to time we may send you information about the work of BRF Ministries. Please contact us if you wish to discuss your mailing preferences **brf.org.uk/privacy**

Please return this form with the appropriate payment to:
BRF Ministries, 15 The Chambers, Vineyard, Abingdon OX14 3FE
For terms and cancellation information, please visit brfonline.org.uk/terms.

Bible Reading Fellowship is a charity (233280) and company limited by guarantee (301324), registered in England and Wales

DIRECT DEBIT PAYMENT

You can pay for your annual subscription to our Bible reading notes using Direct Debit. You need only give your bank details once, and the payment is made automatically every year until you cancel it. If you would like to pay by Direct Debit, please use the form opposite, entering your BRF account number under 'Reference number'.

You are fully covered by the Direct Debit Guarantee:

The Direct Debit Guarantee

- This Guarantee is offered by all banks and building societies that accept instructions to pay Direct Debits.
- If there are any changes to the amount, date or frequency of your Direct Debit, Bible Reading Fellowship will notify you 10 working days in advance of your account being debited or as otherwise agreed. If you request Bible Reading Fellowship to collect a payment, confirmation of the amount and date will be given to you at the time of the request.
- If an error is made in the payment of your Direct Debit, by Bible Reading Fellowship or your bank or building society, you are entitled to a full and immediate refund of the amount paid from your bank or building society.
- If you receive a refund you are not entitled to, you must pay it back when Bible Reading Fellowship asks you to.
- You can cancel a Direct Debit at any time by simply contacting your bank or building society. Written confirmation may be required. Please also notify us.

Instruction to your bank or building society to pay by Direct Debit

Please fill in the whole form using a ballpoint pen and return with order form to:
BRF Ministries, 15 The Chambers, Vineyard, Abingdon OX14 3FE

Service User Number: | 5 | 5 | 8 | 2 | 2 | 9 |

Name and full postal address of your bank or building society

To: The Manager	Bank/Building Society
Address	
	Postcode

Name(s) of account holder(s)

Branch sort code

☐ ☐ – ☐ ☐ – ☐ ☐

Bank/Building Society account number

☐ ☐ ☐ ☐ ☐ ☐ ☐ ☐

Reference number

☐ ☐ ☐ ☐ ☐ ☐ ☐ ☐ ☐ ☐

Instruction to your Bank/Building Society
Please pay Bible Reading Fellowship Direct Debits from the account detailed
in this instruction, subject to the safeguards assured by the Direct Debit Guarantee.
I understand that this instruction may remain with Bible Reading Fellowship
and, if so, details will be passed electronically to my bank/building society.

Signature(s)

Banks and Building Societies may not accept Direct Debit instructions for some
types of account.

BRF Ministries

Inspiring people of all ages to grow in Christian faith

BRF Ministries is the home of Anna Chaplaincy, Living Faith, Messy Church and Parenting for Faith

As a charity, our work would not be possible without fundraising and gifts in wills.
To find out more and to donate,
visit brf.org.uk/give or call +44 (0)1235 462305